Treating the Field as a Lab

A Basic Guide to Conducting Economics Experiments
for Policymaking

ANGELINO C. G. VICEISZA

International Food Policy Research Institute
2033 K Street, NW
Washington, DC 20006-1002
Telephone +1-202-862-5600
www.ifpri.org

DOI: http://dx.doi.org/10.2499/9780896297968

Library of Congress Cataloging-in-Publication Data

Viceisza, Angelino C. G.
Treating the field as a lab : a basic guide to conducting economics
   experiments for policymaking / Angelino C.G. Viceisza.
      p.   cm. — (Food security in practice)
   Includes bibliographical references and index.
   ISBN 978-0-89629-796-8 (pbk. : alk. paper) — ISBN 0-89629-796-9
   (pbk. : alk. paper)
   1. Experimental economics.   2. Economics—Methodology.
   I. International Food Policy Research Institute.   II.   Title.   III. Title:
   Basic guide to conducting economics experiments for policymaking.
   IV. Series: Food security in practice technical guide series.
   HB131.V53 2012
   330.072—dc23
                                                                        2012025532

ABOUT IFPRI

The International Food Policy Research Institute (IFPRI®) was established in 1975 to identify and analyze alternative national and international strategies and policies for meeting food needs of the developing world on a sustainable basis, with particular emphasis on low-income countries and on the poorer groups in those countries. While the research effort is geared to the precise objective of contributing to the reduction of hunger and malnutrition, the factors involved are many and wide-ranging, requiring analysis of underlying processes and extending beyond a narrowly defined food sector. The Institute's research program reflects worldwide collaboration with governments and private and public institutions interested in increasing food production and improving the equity of its distribution. Research results are disseminated to policymakers, opinion formers, administrators, policy analysts, researchers, and others concerned with national and international food and agricultural policy.

IFPRI is a member of the CGIAR Consortium.

ABOUT IFPRI FOOD SECURITY IN PRACTICE

The Food Security in Practice technical guide series is designed for development practitioners. The guides are meant to enrich the research skills of project personnel in the field. Each volume addresses informational and methodological issues that practitioners may confront during the life of a project, explaining relevant research and operational concepts in easy-to-understand ways. All manuscripts submitted for publication as IFPRI technical guides undergo an extensive review procedure that is managed by IFPRI's Publications Review Committee (PRC). Upon submission to the PRC, the manuscript is reviewed by a PRC member. Once the manuscript is considered ready for external review, the PRC submits it to at least two external reviewers who are chosen for their familiarity with the subject matter and the country setting. Upon receipt of these blind external peer reviews, the PRC provides the author with an editorial decision and, when necessary, instructions for revision based on the external reviews. The PRC reassesses the revised manuscript and makes a recommendation regarding publication to the director general of IFPRI. With the director general's approval, the manuscript enters the editorial and production phase to become an IFPRI technical guide.

Contents

Figures and Boxes

Figures

Boxes

Acronyms and Abbreviations

BGT	behavioral game theory
CITI	Collaborative Institutional Training Initiative
DA	double auction
DGP	data-generating process
E	elastic
ESA	Economic Science Association
I	inelastic
IFPRI	International Food Policy Research Institute
IMEEL	IFPRI Mobile Experimental Economics Laboratory
IRB	institutional review board
LAN	local area network
LSMS	Living Standards Measurement Study
NBER	National Bureau of Economic Research
NE	Nash equilibrium
PDA	personal digital assistant
PO	posted offer
PSU	primary sampling unit
RCT	randomized controlled trial
SEEDEC	Symposium on Economic Experiments in Developing Countries
SPNE	subgame perfect Nash equilibrium
SS	sample size

Foreword

Conducting experiments has become a popular tool in economics research. Despite the growing use of the experimental approach, however, the methodology of experimentation has not found its way into the toolkit of the typical economist. In addition, while policymakers are often presented with the results of experimental work, they do not necessarily have the background to understand the rationale for conducting such experiments or an understanding of how the experiments can positively affect policy decisions.

Treating the Field as a Lab: A Basic Guide to Conducting Economics Experiments for Policymaking offers economists, researchers, and policymakers 19 basic principles for conducting experiments in developing-country contexts. In this Food Security in Practice technical guide, Angelino Viceisza focuses on the class of economics experiments known as *lablike field experiments* and examines their basic rationale, the details involved in conducting them, and some of the applications of them in the literature. In addition, Viceisza discusses the role of game theory in conducting field experiments and considers some of the typical issues that can arise when drawing inferences and deriving policy implications from experimental work.

Viceisza also suggests additional topics for future study. One such issue is which methodological difficulties experimenters face most often. For example, is a tendency among participants to alter their behavior because they know they are being studied a major problem? Alternatively, does the manner in which an experiment is framed affect the results? Another important issue for further exploration is the role lablike field experiments can play in future policymaking.

Treating the Field as a Lab responds to a gap in the existing experimental literature by explaining how to conduct lablike field experiments and weighs the strengths and weaknesses of this innovative research method.

SHENGGEN FAN
Director General,
International Food Policy
Research Institute

Acknowledgments

I thank Tanguy Bernard, Gary Charness, Ruth Vargas Hill, Eduardo Maruyama, and Maximo Torero, as well as participants at several conferences, for the meaningful discussions that contributed to the ideas in this guide. My thanks also go to Gershon Feder, the Publications Review Committee of the International Food Policy Research Institute (IFPRI), and two anonymous reviewers for specific comments on how to improve the contents of the guide. I gratefully acknowledge the financial support of the IFPRI Mobile Experimental Economics Laboratory.

CHAPTER I

Introduction

THE TERM *EXPERIMENT* HAS BECOME QUITE POPULAR IN ECONOMICS. Examples of experiments abound in the literature of many subfields of economics, in particular experimental, behavioral, and development economics.[1] Despite the growing use of the term *experiment* and of the experimental approach in economics, the methodology of experimentation has not yet found its way into the typical economist's (and researcher's) toolkit. In addition, although many policymakers are faced with inferences drawn from experimental work, they do not necessarily possess a proper insight as to why and how one conducts experiments and what the strengths and weaknesses of the approach are.

The purpose of this guide is to bridge the divide between those who are familiar with experiments and those who are less so but have an interest in either conducting experiments or using the literature. Therefore, the scope of this guide is relatively practical, concise, and limited. It is not a complete discussion of experimental methodology, its applications, or the literature. Rather it is a specific discussion of some concepts and issues that are useful to know in order to be able to conduct or understand experiments, particularly when drawing inferences for policy.

It is useful to discuss what the term *experiment* means for our purposes. Generally, an experiment can be seen as a set of observations generated in a controlled environment in the context of answering a particular question or solving a particular problem. This guide focuses on the class of *lablike field experiments* in economics. In the taxonomy of Harrison and List (2004), the lablike field experiments considered here comprise so-called artefactual field experiments and certain framed field experiments. This guide does not, however, focus on so-called randomized controlled trials (RCTs), which, depending on their design, can be considered framed field experiments. The experiments considered distinguish themselves from typical laboratory experiments in that they are conducted with nonstudent subject pools. It is in this sense that they are considered *field* experiments. However, they also distinguish themselves from RCTs and so-called natural field experiments

---

[1] The field of experimental economics can be seen as the application of experimental methods to questions in economics. The field of behavioral economics can be seen as the use of social, cognitive, and emotional factors in understanding the economic decisions of individuals and institutions performing economic functions.

in that subjects make decisions that are not necessarily part of their day-to-day decisionmaking (typically in a game environment), know that they are part of an experiment, or both.

The main reasoning for limiting the focus of this guide is the following. Within the taxonomy of field experiments, natural field experiments tend to be the most complicated to implement. Therefore, it does not seem appropriate to try to address this class of field experiments to a sufficient extent in this guide. This said, many of the issues addressed in this guide are also applicable to such experiments. With regard to RCTs, a book chapter by Duflo, Glennerster, and Kremer (2007) is a useful starting point for those who are interested in conducting such experiments. So the literature is not at a loss if these experiments are not adequately addressed in this guide.

To further understand the purposes of lablike field experiments, particularly for policymaking, it makes sense to go back to the basic rationale for conducting (economic) research. A meaningful way to think about the process of research is to break it down into the following stages (see Mookherjee 2005, based on Haavelmo 1958):

1. **Stage 1.** Empirical description of the relevant phenomenon, consisting of exploratory data analysis aimed at helping identify empirical regularities that need to be explained by a suitable theory and, in addition, the nature of assumptions that such a theory can make without gross violation of the empirical patterns.

2. **Stage 2.** The formulation of a relevant theory, including derivation of potentially observable (hence falsifiable) implications.

3. **Stage 3.** The estimation and testing of theories, a stage that may lead back to modification or replacement of the previous theories in an iterative back-and-forth process with Stage 2.

4. **Stage 4.** Use of the least unsuccessful theory—from the standpoint of empirical verification—for purposes of prediction and policy implementation and evaluation.

So ultimately the research process informs policymaking.[2] It is in the process of generating (collecting) data to test theories and inform policy that experiments can serve a very useful purpose.

Friedman and Sunder (1994, 3) comment that "data for empirical work can be drawn from several types of sources, each with distinctive

---

[2] As Friedman and Sunder (1994) indicate, the alternation of theory and empirical work, each refining the other, is the engine of progress in every scientific discipline. Samuelson (2005) discusses the interactions between theory and experiments in particular.

characteristics, advantages, and disadvantages. A key distinction is between *experimental data* which are deliberately created for scientific (or other) purposes under *controlled* conditions, and *happenstance data,* which are a byproduct of ongoing *uncontrolled* processes" (emphasis in original).[3] Indeed, one of the most appealing features of experimental data, and of the experimental approach more broadly, is that they enable the experimenter or econometrician to have a relatively high degree of control over the data-generating process and therefore to be able to isolate the main effect of interest.

Lablike field experiments have primarily been conducted with three purposes in mind that are not mutually exclusive:

1. To test theories or heuristic principles.

2. To measure what have traditionally been considered "unobservable" characteristics.

3. To test the sensitivity of experimental results (possibly resulting from 1 or 2) to different forms of heterogeneity (such as variations in the subject population, alternative institutions, and so on).

These three purposes are closely tied to the role of lablike field experiments in informing policymaking. Chapter 3 discusses sample experiments in detail while linking them to the policymaking process. So some brief motivation is provided in the following.

Lablike field experiments have been used to test theories or heuristic principles that have implications for policy. Two examples are Giné et al. (2010) and Hill and Viceisza (2012). Giné et al. created a laboratory in a large urban market in Lima, Peru, and conducted framed field experiments (in the terminology of Harrison and List 2004) to unpack microfinance mechanisms in a systematic way. They found that risk taking broadly conforms to theoretical predictions and that, although group lending can facilitate profitable risk taking (while maintaining high rates of loan repayment), the costs tend to be borne by fellow borrowers and fall most heavily on the risk averse. Their findings have implications for the design of microfinance arrangements and suggest factors that policymakers and nongovernmental organizations should take into account when designing such schemes, particularly because the risk averse are also more likely to be otherwise deprived.

Hill and Viceisza created a laboratory in a village in rural Ethiopia to understand the determinants of investment behavior with regard to a risky

---

[3]Friedman, D., and S. Sunder. 1994. *Experimental Methods: A Primer for Economists.* Cambridge, UK: Cambridge University Press. Copyright © 1994 Cambridge University Press. Reprinted with the permission of Cambridge University Press.

asset such as fertilizer. Specifically, we devised a framed field experiment to test the seminal hypothesis that insurance induces farmers to take greater, yet profitable risks (along the lines of Sandmo 1971). We found that although insurance has some positive effect on fertilizer purchases, weather expectations (as proxied by prior weather shocks) play a more prominent role in determining investment behavior. Our findings complement the policy hypothesis that posits insurance as a means to promote investment and growth through greater profitable risk taking. The findings also suggest that it is important to take people's historical experiences into account when implementing new policies and programs.

A main feature of experiments that makes them a great tool for testing theories, heuristics, and mechanisms is that they enable us to construct a proper counterfactual scenario for establishing causality, and thus for identifying effects. This goes back to the issue of control raised previously. For example, in both of the aforementioned examples, behavior in modified treatments was compared to behavior in baseline or control treatments ("the counterfactual") in order to test certain hypotheses, in particular to identify a treatment effect.

As Harrison and List (2004, 1014) indicate, "The goal of any evaluation method for treatment effects is to construct the proper counterfactual. Define y_1 as the outcome with treatment, y_0 as the outcome without treatment and let $T = 1$ when treated and $T = 0$ when not treated. Then, the treatment effect for unit i can be measured as $\tau_i = y_{i1} - y_{i0}$." For example, in the Hill and Viceisza (2012) example discussed previously, the treatment (T) was the provision of insurance and the outcome (y_r) was the number of bags of fertilizer purchased.

The counterfactual, τ_i, is not known, however. In other words, if we observe individual i in one scenario, we do not observe the same individual in a different scenario at the same time. Harrison and List (2004, 1014) note: "If we could observe the outcome for an untreated observation had it been treated, then there would be no evaluation problem.[4] Controlled experiments, which include laboratory and field experiments, represent the most convincing method of creating the counterfactual, since they directly construct a control group via randomization." In other words, they constructed a "comparable" comparison group by assigning random subsamples of a population to be treated or not. They go on to say that "in this

---

[4] Notice that even with a within-subjects design in which we observe the same individual in one condition (possibly a control) at point $t = 0$ and in a different condition (possibly a treatment) at point $t = 1$, we do not get rid of the evaluation problem. Namely, the fact that the individual has already experienced one condition by the time she arrives at point $t = 1$ makes her situation different than if we were to observe her *at the same point in time in both conditions* [footnote added].

case, the population *average* treatment effect is given by $\tau = y_1^* - y_0^*$, where y_1^* and y_0^* are treated and nontreated average outcomes after the treatment" (1014–1015 [emphasis added]). This is typically the main effect of interest when we conduct an experiment for purposes of evaluating a particular treatment (see also Wooldridge 2002 for a more general discussion on treatment effects).

Although experiments may be the most convincing way to create a proper counterfactual and thus identify a treatment effect of interest, they are not the only way. Indeed, Wooldridge (2002); Duflo, Glennerster, and Kremer (2007); and Harrison and List (2004) all discuss alternative quasi- or nonexperimental approaches to impact evaluation, such as natural experiments, difference-in-difference, matching, instrumental variables estimation, regression discontinuity, and structural methods.[5]

Lablike field experiments have also been used to elicit characteristics that have traditionally been considered "unobservable," such as preferences and beliefs. For example, consider a lottery choice experiment for eliciting time preferences. The typical purpose of such an experiment is to elicit a characteristic of interest.[6] Of course this characteristic may be used as a control when further disentangling the effect of a treatment ex post (this is the third role for these experiments, which is considered next); however, the main purpose of the lottery choice experiment is elicitation and not identification per se. These experiments are useful because they enable us to capture aspects that, if not carefully accounted for, can lead to spurious policy implications. Consider the example of technology adoption, a major issue in development. There is evidence to suggest that a major determinant of people's propensity to adopt a technology is their risk preference (see, for example, Engle-Warnick, Escobal, and Laszlo 2011 for the case of agricultural technologies). So having a proper risk preference measure, such as one elicited through a lablike field experiment, is important (we return to this issue when discussing risk and time experiments).

The use of lablike field experiments to measure unobservables is not unique to risk preferences. The same usage applies to time preferences; propensities to trust, coordinate, or cooperate; beliefs (for example, regarding the weather); and so on. Although from a policy standpoint it may be difficult to change people's preferences or beliefs (or both), having such

---

[5] See Khandker, Koolwal, and Samad (2010) for additional discussion on program evaluation methods and applications. The June 2010 issue of the *Journal of Economic Literature* and the summer 2011 issue of the *Journal of Economic Perspectives* contain some "must-read" articles for those more deeply interested in experimental methodology and the strengths and weaknesses of the approach relative to others.

[6] As we shall discuss later, some lottery choice experiments are specifically designed to test the plausibility of models of choice under uncertainty such as expected utility.

information can still help policymakers design more effective institutions and programs. For example, when introducing a new technology as part of a program, it might make sense to combine the program with an insurance package that limits the downside risk from irreversible investment and thereby guarantees that the most risk-averse participants opt in.

The third purpose of lablike field experiments is tied to the former. Suppose we conduct lablike field experiments to test a particular theory and find a given effect. For example, in the case of Hill and Viceisza (2012), we found that insurance had a slightly positive effect on ex ante risk taking. We can now ask to what extent this effect varies with risk aversion. In other words, are the risk averse more likely to react positively to the introduction of insurance? We can use experiments of type 2 to further disentangle the effects found in experiments of type 1. In other words, we can combine the two primary purposes of experiments to further understand behavioral mechanisms. These refinements, in turn, enable us to design more precise programs and policies.

This third purpose is unique neither to refinements of preferences and beliefs nor to refinements of lablike field experimental results. Consider the first claim. Lablike field experiments also enable us to test the robustness of treatment effects to alternative institutions, not just preferences and beliefs. For example, by designing additional treatments that may not be of primary interest (such as variations on the insurance product), we can further understand the institutional mechanisms underlying certain effects as opposed to just behavioral mechanisms.

Next, consider the second claim. Lablike field experiments also enable us to understand mechanisms underlying effects that result from other types of experiments, in particular RCTs. For example, suppose an actual intervention is conducted in which different types of technologies are randomly offered to farmers and take-up is studied. We can use risk and time preferences elicited through lablike field experiments to test whether take-up varies with these aspects. We can perform a similar exercise with other measures such as trust, beliefs, and so on. In fact, many studies that seek to inform policymaking nowadays pair RCTs with lablike field experiments (as well as other methods) in order to garner a better understanding of the mechanisms involved. Some examples include Barr, Packard, and Serra (2011), Jamison and Karlan (2011), and the IFPRI project Working Together for Market Access: Strengthening Rural Producer Organizations in Sub-Saharan Africa.[7] All of these studies combine data from lablike field

---

[7] The purpose of this project is to study the ability of rural producer organizations (farmer groups) to provide services (in particular, marketing) to their members and the role of internal group dynamics in achieving the organization's goals. The project focuses on Senegal and Uganda.

experiments with data from RCTs (along with other sources of data such as surveys).

There is a final pedagogical purpose for lablike field experiments that has been highlighted by Friedman and Sunder (1994) for the standard classroom but also noted *anecdotally* based on the work reported by Carter (2008) and Hill and Viceisza (2012) for experiments conducted in developing-country contexts. Experiments can serve the meaningful purpose of demonstrating economic propositions and concepts to those who are less familiar with them. Both Carter and Hill and Viceisza have noted that experiments served a meaningful purpose in explaining complex index-based insurance contracts to less educated rural farmers. By having subjects play simple games that mimic their day-to-day environment in essential ways and introducing slight variations thereto, one can use experiments to explain complex concepts. To the best of our knowledge, there have been no studies that have designed experiments with this as their main purpose.

The remainder of the guide is organized as follows. Next, we discuss the details of experimentation—that is, how we go about designing and implementing lablike field experiments. Readers who are not interested in conducting experiments can skip this chapter. We then discuss some common field experiments that have been observed in the literature. In the process, we will also review some basic concepts in the theory of games and economic behavior and the role of theory in conducting experiments. We then address some typical issues that arise when drawing inferences and deriving policy implications from (field) experiments. Finally, we conclude by taking a forward-looking perspective on some open questions that remain in the literature on lablike field experiments.

Prior to proceeding to the next chapter, we list selected additional reading that may be of interest to those wanting to dig deeper into experimental methodologies (in economics). Some of this, as well as additional work, will be referenced in greater detail as we move through the guide. These references are Davis and Holt (1993), Kagel and Roth (1997), Cox and Reid (2000), Camerer (2003), Caplin and Schotter (2008), Cox and Harrison (2008), Plott and Smith (2008), Falk and Heckman (2009), Fréchette and Schotter (forthcoming), and certain articles in the June 2010 and summer 2011 issues of the *Journal of Economic Literature* and the *Journal of Economic Perspectives,* respectively.

CHAPTER 2
How to Experiment

I N THIS CHAPTER WE DISCUSS HOW ONE GOES ABOUT EXPERIMENTING. FOR those wanting to conduct experiments, this is one of the most important chapters in this guide. Readers who are not necessarily interested in conducting experiments, however, can skip this chapter. Some of what we discuss here is mainly taken from Friedman and Sunder (1994); the interested reader is referred to their text for further discussion (see also List 2011 for some related discussion). The chapter sums up the discussion of each aspect of experimentation in the form of a practical principle. Potential experimenters can use these principles as necessary (but not sufficient) guidelines for conducting an experiment (for summaries of the principles, see Boxes 2.1–2.5, placed at strategic points throughout this chapter). As mentioned previously, one of the main features of (economics) experiments is control. To have control (in this context) means that the experimenter, by design of the data collection, can control the data-generating process and thus be able to make inferences more easily than would be the case using happenstance data. The recurring theme of this chapter will be achieving or maintaining (experimenter) control.

We start by discussing the basic issues related to how an experimenter gains control over the experimental environment. Then we address different premises for experimental design, after which we turn to the main considerations that factor into constructing a proper experiment protocol and implementing the experimental design. Finally, this chapter concludes with a discussion of some practical issues that should be kept in mind when conducting an experiment.

BASIC ISSUES

The first principle for experimentation is to formulate a proper research question and purpose. The reason this is important is that it determines the appropriateness of the experimental design and treatments under consideration. In other words, what may be a brilliant experimental design in one context may be completely inappropriate in another context *because of the research question under consideration*. This is a first principle for research more broadly as well.

For illustrative purposes, consider the example of a *market experiment*. A conventional laboratory market experiment entails a group of 20–40 participants (recruited by the experimenter) gathered at a specific location (typically, an experimental laboratory) to engage in trade of artefactual commodities. The participants are usually divided into buyers and sellers, and the experimenter induces certain conditions and rules under which trade is valid or becomes binding.[1] At the end of the experiment, participants are paid their earnings for the experiment in cash, thus giving them an incentive to (1) understand the rules of the experiment and (2) behave as profit-maximizing agents tend to do in naturally occurring markets.

The typical purpose for such a market experiment is to test whether actual behavior conforms to theoretical predictions. For example, we may want to study to what extent equilibrium is reached if behavior is studied across different market institutions. If this is our primary research question of interest, we can randomly assign participants to different types of institutions and study their behavior across these distinct treatment conditions. On the other hand, suppose we want to study to what extent agents reach equilibrium if the initial conditions are different, for example, if the seller's reservation prices are above a certain threshold. Because the research question is different, our treatment conditions should be different as well. With this question in mind, we can hold the market institution fixed and randomly assign participants to different thresholds. The take-away from this example is that one's experimental design should be guided by the main question under consideration. If not, this will typically lead to badly designed experiments.[2]

So the first principle for experimentation is:

PRINCIPLE 1   Clearly define the research question and purpose of interest.

The second principle is to develop a conceptual framework (or theoretical model) for designing the experiment treatments. This is closely related to stage 2 of Mookherjee's characterization, discussed in the previous section. In other words, it is useful to have a framework in place (or in mind) that in some relevant manner describes how subjects might behave as part of one's experiment. This framework typically predicts behavior in the baseline and main treatment(s) of interest. For example, in the market

---

[1] This is a deliberately simplified description of a market experiment. Later sections discuss how we would go about designing and implementing such an experiment.

[2] Notice that these research questions are not mutually exclusive. In particular, we can conduct additional treatments that enable us to study the effect of higher reservation prices across different market institutions. One way to achieve this would be by means of a so-called factorial design, a concept that I discuss later.

experiments described previously, such a framework might be a standard supply-and-demand model or some type of auction mechanism.

Seminal papers such as those by Smith (1976, 1982) and Plott (1982) provide a generic discussion of the key methods for creating a controlled economic environment in the laboratory. To a great extent, these methods apply to the field as well. They start from the premise that economic behavior takes place in an economic system. In particular, "a microeconomic system is a complete, self-contained economy [that] consists of a set of *agents* and the *institutions* through which they interact" (Friedman and Cassar 2004, 25 [emphasis added]).[3] Friedman and Sunder (1994, 12) explain that "agents are defined by their economically relevant characteristics": preferences and constraints (technological, resource, and informational), "whereas, an economic institution specifies the actions available to agents and the outcomes that result from each possible combination of agents' actions."[4]

To study behavior in a controlled environment, the experimenter must thus be able to "control" the agents, the institution(s) through which they interact, or both. The extent to which the experimenter wants to control either of these depends on the research question. It also depends on whether the experimenter wants the experimental environment to parallel certain aspects of the naturally occurring environment. For example, subjects (that is, the actual agents in an experiment) have their own homegrown characteristics. Sometimes the experimenter may want to elicit those, and other times she may want to examine theories or hypotheses that take those characteristics as given. Achieving experimental control over the institution is conceptually straightforward relative to controlling subjects' characteristics: The experimenter need only explain and enforce the rules associated with the specific institution in question. On the other hand, controlling agent or subject characteristics is not so straightforward. Friedman and Sunder (1994) discuss how such control is achieved; the following discussion is drawn from their work.

One method of control examined by Friedman and Sunder is *induced value theory* (a concept proposed in Smith 1976). The key idea is that proper use of a reward medium allows an experimenter to induce pre-specified characteristics in experimental subjects such that the subjects' innate characteristics become largely irrelevant. Three conditions are sufficient to induce agents' characteristics:

---

[3] This description can apply with equal validity to theoretical models, naturally occurring economies (large and small), and artefactual economies in the laboratory (Friedman and Cassar 2004). So we can think of such characterization as being relevant to lablike field experiments but also to RCTs.

[4] Friedman, D., and S. Sunder. 1994. *Experimental Methods: A Primer for Economists.* Cambridge, UK: Cambridge University Press. Copyright © 1994 Cambridge University Press. Reprinted with the permission of Cambridge University Press.

1. **Monotonicity.** Subjects must prefer more of the reward medium to less and not become satiated. Formally, if $V(m, z)$ represents the subjects' unobservable preferences over the reward medium (m) and everything else (z), the monotonicity condition is that the partial derivative with respect to the reward medium (V_m) exist and be positive for every feasible combination of (m, z). This condition is typically satisfied by using a subject's domestic currency ("money") as the reward medium.

2. **Salience.** The reward Δm received by the subject depends on her actions (and those of other agents) as defined by institutional rules that she understands. In other words, the relation between actions and the reward implements the desired institution, and subjects understand the relation. For example, a $5.00 fixed payment to subjects for participating in an experiment would not satisfy salience according to the given definition because the payment would not depend on the subjects' choice of actions during the experiment.

3. **Dominance.** Changes in subjects' utility from the experiment come predominantly from the reward medium, and other influences are negligible. This condition is the most problematic, because preferences V and "everything else" z may not be observable by the experimenter. Dominance becomes more plausible if the salient rewards Δm are increased (this is usually why experimentalists report how average earnings in an experiment rank relative to subjects' day-to-day earnings) and if the more obvious components of z are held constant. For example, subjects often care about the rewards earned by other subjects. If the experimental procedures make it impossible to know or estimate others' rewards (Smith calls this "privacy"), a component of z is neutralized.[5]

Typically, the best the experimenter can do is to mitigate this effect during the experiment. After the experiment, it is impossible to control the extent to which subjects interact and discuss earnings. This is particularly true in rural field contexts in which we may expect subjects to know each other and be more likely to have discussions after the experiment. Another example is experimenter demand effects, which arise from subjects' efforts to help (or hinder) the experimenter. The experimenter can try to mitigate such effects by revealing as little as possible about the goals of the experiment. We return to the discussion of such complexities later.

---

5 Ibid.

So the second principle for conducting an experiment is:

PRINCIPLE 2 Develop a theoretical or conceptual framework that informs those components of an experiment that need to be controlled. Generally such components are agents' characteristics (preferences and constraints), the institutions through which agents interact, or both.

The third principle for experimentation has to do with the "realism" of the task at hand. Some have questioned the external validity of experimental environments. This brings us to the notion of parallelism. Smith (1982) refers to the parallelism precept as follows: propositions about the behavior of individuals and the performance of institutions that have been tested in "laboratory" microeconomies apply also to "nonlaboratory" microeconomies *where similar ceteris paribus conditions hold.*

Friedman and Sunder (1994) have made useful comments on this topic. According to parallelism, they observe, it should be presumed that results carry over to the world outside the laboratory. It is then up to a skeptic to point out things that are different in the outside world that may change the results observed in the laboratory. Usually new experiments can be designed and conducted to test the skeptic's statement. The idea is to use such skepticism to promote constructive research and not to engage in sterile arguments. Parallelism relies on *induction* as a maintained hypothesis. The general idea of induction is that behavioral regularities will persist in new situations as long as the relevant underlying conditions remain substantially unchanged. Typically, theory suggests what is "relevant" and what is "substantial" change.[6]

This insight is important for numerous reasons. First, it reiterates the importance of principle 2—the development of a theoretical framework that not only guides the design of the experiment but also generalization of the main results. Second, it illustrates the importance of developing a framework that captures the most relevant aspects of agents' decisionmaking environment. This is particularly important when conducting lablike field experiments in developing countries (that is, experiments with poor subjects) where certain constraints (such as liquidity, credit, and savings) may be highly prevalent in the day-to-day environment. Failure to properly account for them can lead to poorly designed experiments, incorrect inferences, or both.

Finally, this insight raises the question how does one respond when someone disclaims one's experiment as too far removed from reality? First and foremost, the extent to which external validity is of major concern depends

---

[6]Ibid.

on the purpose and the research question of the experiment. For example, these issues tend to be of less concern when conducting experiments to test theory.[7] After all, most theories are silent as to the types of agents (read: types of people, be they students, farmers, policymakers, women, or men) to which they are applicable. As Camerer (2011) argues, generalizability need not be of primary concern in a typical experiment, and, to the extent that it is, there are many studies showing "lab"–field generalizability.

To the extent that we are concerned about external validity given the experiment at hand, researchers have attempted to deal with the issue in the following ways. First, several researchers have complemented the experiment(s) with a detailed survey that collects data on many types of observables in addition to the experimental data of interest. For example, suppose one does not attempt to mimic liquidity constraints as part of one's experiment. In such a case, one may test whether a liquidity proxy constructed from one's survey data has any predictive power over either the main variable or the treatment variable of interest.

Second, researchers may actually design additional experiment treatments. Although this is the most ideal way to go, this is typically the most costly, in terms of both time and monetary costs. Therefore, it is often infeasible. As a result, it is important to carefully design one's experiment ex ante considering the most relevant issues. One such issue may be framing, a topic we return to later. We return to issues related to external validity in Chapter 4.

So the third principle in conducting an experiment is:

PRINCIPLE 3 Depending on the purpose of the experiment, consider parallelism. Design the experiment considering the most relevant components of the agents' day-to-day decisionmaking environment.

EXPERIMENTAL DESIGN

The previous discussion on identifying the most relevant components of agents' day-to-day decisionmaking environment leads nicely to the topic of experimental design.[8] Friedman and Sunder (1994) observe that in any experiment we are typically interested in the effects of only a few variables, the so-called *focus* variables. These focus variables can usually be divided into outcome and treatment variables. An outcome variable is a main

---

[7] As Falk and Heckman (2009) discuss, lablike experiments are very powerful whenever tight control of nuisance factors is essential.

[8] This section on experimental design draws heavily on Friedman and Sunder (1994). For a more detailed treatment on the theory of the design of experiments, see Cox and Reid (2000).

BOX 2.1   Principles for designing an experiment: Basic issues

1. Clearly define the research question and the experiment's purpose.

2. Develop a conceptual framework to account for the components of the experiment that need to be controlled. Such components might be agents' characteristics, the institutions through which agents interact, or both.

3. Depending on the experiment's purpose, incorporate the most relevant components of the agents' real-life decisionmaking environment into the experiment's design.

Source: Author.

---

variable of interest. In an "identification" experiment, this is the variable we use to test for impact (in a regression context, this would be the dependent variable). A treatment variable is what we plan to vary by the design of our experiment in order to identify the impact on the outcome variable (in a regression context, this would be the main independent variable).[9]

Although our main interest may be on the focus variables, usually we must also keep track of several other variables that are of little or no direct interest but that may affect our results, the so-called *nuisance* variables. The distinction between focus and nuisance variables is determined by the purpose of the experiment. Our discussion in this section seeks to address how to design experiments that sharpen the effects of focus variables and minimize the confounding of results due to nuisance variables.[10]

So the fourth principle for conducting an experiment is:

PRINCIPLE 4 Identify the focus (outcome and treatment) variables and the nuisance variables.

Direct experimental control: Constants and treatments

By controlling important variables, Friedman and Sunder (1994) explain, we produce experimental data rather than happenstance data. The simplest way to control a variable is to hold it *constant* at some convenient level. For example, in the market experiment discussed previously, the experimenter

---

[9]In an "elicitation" experiment, the outcome variable is the main variable that we typically seek to uncover. Some examples are preferences for risk, time, altruism, and so on.

[10]Friedman and Sunder, *Experimental Methods.* Copyright © 1994 Cambridge University Press. Reprinted with the permission of Cambridge University Press.

may choose to enforce the same double-auction trading rules throughout the experiment. The main alternative is to choose two or more distinct levels that may produce sharply different outcomes and to control the variable at each chosen level for part of the experiment (or subset of experiments). Perhaps because of their prevalence in medical experiments, variables controlled at two or more levels are called *treatment* variables.

There is a trade-off between controlling variables as constants and as treatments. As we hold more variables constant, the experiment becomes simpler and cheaper, but we learn less about the direct effects and the interactions among the variables. Suppose we choose two treatment variables, say the market institution with levels PO (posted offer) and DA (double auction) and the demand elasticity with levels E (elastic) and I (inelastic).

Despite control, we will completely confound the effects of these variables if we always change them together, using, say, a PO-E combination half the time and a DA-I combination the other half. Instead, if we adopt a 2 × 2 design by running each treatment combination (PO-E, PO-I, DA-E, and DA-I) one-quarter of the time, we can gauge the separate effects of the two treatments. The logic is quite general: *vary all treatment variables independently* to obtain the clearest possible evidence of their effects.[11]

So, the fifth principle for conducting an experiment is:

> **PRINCIPLE 5** Vary the treatment variables independently. Some focus variables may be held constant—this is a special case of a "treatment."

Indirect control: Randomization

Friedman and Sunder (1994) also discuss the fact that certain variables are difficult or impossible to control. Consider, for example, subjects' expectations, alertness, interest, and other unobservable characteristics. More important, even if we are able to elicit certain variables and thus control them, we may not want to, because it may be costly to do so and they are nuisance (as opposed to focus) variables.[12] To the extent possible, we should design additional treatments to assess potential confounding effects or disentangle behavioral mechanisms. For example, we can employ

---

[11]Ibid.

[12]Ibid. Typically, we can expect the following effects to confound the treatment: (1) historical and learning effects, (2) endowment effects, (3) Hawthorne and demand effects (see, for example, Zwane et al. 2011), (4) social and peer effects, (5) external or homegrown preference and constraint effects, and (6) calibration effects. These uncontrolled nuisances can cause inferential errors if they are confounded with focus variables. Furthermore, they can also lead to a "zero" treatment effect because they can introduce noise.

difference-in-difference designs to wipe out historical and learning effects, between-subject designs to mitigate experimenter demand effects across treatments (more on this later), randomized seating and dividers to mitigate social effects or more elaborate treatments in which subjects observe decisions made by peers prior to their own decisionmaking, and rationale or hypothetical questions to better understand the process that underlies subjects' decisionmaking.

Realistically, however, it is likely that neither time nor budget will allow for additional treatments to test all of these effects. So one should plan for a way to indirectly control these nuisances ex ante (by design) or to assess these ex post through econometric analysis, whether or not supplementary treatments have been designed.

One ex post approach is to elicit responses in a postsurvey that are similar to decisions made in the experimental task but subject to alternative scenarios. These questions can be seen as providing stated-preference data that iterate the revealed preference data collected in the experiment.[13] Another approach is to incorporate qualitative "rationale" questions into one's design. One question might be why did you make a particular decision? An example of such a question was included in the remittance experiments reported by Torero and Viceisza (2012) and in the coordination experiments conducted in the Senegal component of the Working Together for Market Access project, which was discussed in Chapter 1. According to Friedman and Sunder (1994), ex ante *randomization* provides indirect control of uncontrolled or unobservable variables by ensuring the eventual independence of treatment and nuisance variables. The basic idea is to assign chosen levels of the treatment variables in random order.

The primary experimental design in this case is called *completely randomized*. In this design, each treatment (or each conjunction of treatment variables) is equally likely to be assigned in each trial, where a trial is an indivisible unit of an experiment, such as a trading period in a market experiment. Complete randomization is quite effective when you can afford to run many trials.

When *uncontrollable* (*uncontrolled*) nuisances produce little variation across trials, the completely randomized design is hard to improve on. When controllable nuisances do significantly affect outcomes, however, designs that appropriately combine control with randomization are more efficient in the sense that they can produce equally decisive results from fewer trials.

---

[13]In this case, the Train and Wilson (2008) critique for combining revealed and stated preference data should be kept in mind when conducting ex post analysis.

Random block is the general name given to this improved design. The difference from the completely randomized design is that one or more nuisance variables are controlled as treatments rather than randomized. Nuisance treatment variables are often called blocking variables and are held constant within a block (subset of trials) but varied across blocks.

A typical example of a random block design is what is usually referred to as a *within-subjects* design in experimental economics. A within-subjects design varies the level of the focus variable for each subject and thus enables the experimenter to control individual-level nuisances by observing the same subject under different treatment conditions in random order.

The within-subjects design stands in contrast to the *between-subjects* design, which varies the level of the focus variable only *across* subjects. In other words, in a between-subjects design, we observe each subject in only one treatment condition.[14]

The benefit of a within-subjects design is that it enables the experimenter to control individual-level nuisances by comparing outcomes for varying treatment levels for the same subject. Thus, the experimenter can more easily attribute differences in the outcome variable of interest to the treatment (that is, the varying focus variable) as opposed to confounding nuisance variables. For example, if one observes the same subject in treatments A and B, it is unlikely that the subject's expectations (or innate unobservable characteristics more broadly) are confounding the effect of any focus (treatment) variable.

However, a within-subjects design may introduce other potential confounding nuisances into the analysis. The main concern is typically one of order or learning effects. The fact that the same subject participates in varying treatment conditions may lead him to exhibit different behavior across treatments, not because of the change in the focus variable but rather due to subject learning. To avoid such potential nuisances, one can employ a so-called crossover design, which varies the levels of a treatment variable across trials for a subject or group of subjects. For example, one subset of subjects may participate in an ABA ordering of treatments and another subset in a BAB ordering.

The benefit of a between-subjects design is that it mitigates spillover effects across treatments because each subject participates in only one treatment—that is, either A or B. However, this also introduces the complication that uncontrollable nuisance factors such as individual-specific unobservable characteristics may confound the treatment effect. So it is important that there be careful randomization of subjects to treatments

[14]Friedman and Sunder, *Experimental Methods.* Copyright © 1994 Cambridge University Press. Reprinted with the permission of Cambridge University Press.

when employing a between-subjects design in order to avoid any type of "selection." Also, one typically needs a larger overall sample size.

Friedman and Sunder (1994) identified a general method for combining randomization and direct control when you have two or more treatment variables: the *factorial design* (this was previously alluded to in the mention of a 2 × 2 design and when discussing combination of treatments). To illustrate, consider two treatment variables labeled *R* and *S,* with three levels *H, M,* and *L* for *R* and two levels, *H* and *L,* for *S.* In the resulting 3 × 2 factorial design, each of the six treatments *LL, LH, ML, MH, HL,* and *HH* is employed in the same number of *k* trials. Thus 24 trials (3 × 2 × 4) are required to replicate the design *k* = 4 times. Randomization plays an important role, because we must assign the six treatments in random order to the six trials in each replication.[15]

Bruhn and McKenzie (2009) discuss ways of checking *prior* to conducting an experiment (that is, conducting pre-checks) whether randomization was successful. The general concern is that if the sample sizes under consideration are not sufficiently large, randomization may still result in unbalanced samples. Behrman and Todd (1999) discuss ways of checking *after* conducting the experiment (that is, conducting postchecks) whether randomization was successful and, if not, how to incorporate that into the analysis. We return to these issues in Chapter 4.

So the sixth principle for conducting an experiment is:

PRINCIPLE 6 Use randomization or another more elaborate experimental design as an ex ante tool to indirectly control unobservable characteristics, specifically nuisance variables, and thus rule out potential confounding of treatment effects. Use additional, possibly stated-preference, data collected after the experiments to test for possible confounding effects.

EXPERIMENT PROTOCOL: "IT'S ALL ABOUT THE DETAILS"

The previous section was concerned with how to achieve experimental control by design of the experiment. However, it did not say much about how to actually conduct an experiment. This section and the next are concerned with how to maintain control once we actually *implement* the experiment.

Perhaps the best way to think about an experiment protocol is as follows. Suppose we have identified our experimental treatments based on the

---

[15]Ibid.

> **BOX 2.2   Principles for designing an experiment: Experimental design**
>
> 1. Identify the variables of direct interest (the focus variables): the experiment's result ("outcome variable") and the experiment element changed to alter the result ("treatment variable"). Also identify variables that are not of direct interest but might affect the results ("nuisance variables").
>
> 2. Vary the treatment variables independently of one another; this provides the clearest possible evidence of their effects. You might hold some focus variables constant throughout the experiment.
>
> 3. Control for nuisance variables that might interfere with measuring the treatment variables' effects. One approach is to use a more elaborate experimental design in which a treatment variable is randomly applied to sufficiently large subgroups of the population of interest and so cancels out the effects of nuisance variables. A complementary approach is to collect additional data after the experiment. A survey of the experiment subjects, for example, might reveal differences among them that could be the cause of differing outcomes rather than the treatment variable.
>
> **Source:** Author.

"exercise" in the previous section. Each treatment now needs to be implemented. The experiment protocol tells us how to do that. Specifically, the experiment protocol tells us what needs to happen once the experiment is taking place—that is, what process is to be followed once subjects arrive, how they are to be seated, what tasks they will be performing, how they will be paid, and so on. So in the process of formulating an experiment protocol, many questions need to be answered and issues addressed.

Institutional review boards and informed consent

Prior to conducting an experiment, it is important to obtain approval for one's protocol from the institutional review board (IRB) of one's organization, also known as a human subject committee. Most academic or research organizations (including IFPRI) have a committee that oversees human subject research, whose primary purpose is to evaluate the potential risks and benefits that human subjects face as a result of research.

It has been a tradition in experimental economics (a norm adopted primarily from the medical field and from psychology) to submit one's protocol for IRB approval prior to its implementation. Among others, researchers are expected to perform the following steps:

1. Participate in the Collaborative Institutional Training Initiative (CITI) program (www.citiprogram.org/).

2. Submit their experiment protocol for review by the IRB.

3. Obtain approval for or a waiver of informed consent by the IRB.

It is also important that those who are conducting research in countries other than the United States (specifically, developing or transition countries) verify whether additional IRB or third-party approval is necessary prior to conducting an experiment. For example, in some cases the local government authorities or implementing partners may require additional review, either by their own members or by the IRB of a local university.

So the seventh principle for conducting an experiment is:

> **PRINCIPLE 7** Obtain CITI certification and submit your experiment protocol to the IRB for review. Consult any local authorities as necessary.

Obviously, prior to submitting one's protocol for review, it needs to be developed. The first premise for developing an experiment protocol, which ties into our previous comments on defining a research question and achieving or maintaining experimenter control, is to keep it simple. In other words, make sure that the task your subjects are faced with is as simple as possible given the question you would like to address. If you find yourself formulating a very complicated protocol and your justification is that the research question requires it, you will probably find it worth revisiting the research question. For example, the question may be able to be broken down into multiple experiments.

So the eighth principle for conducting an experiment is:

> **PRINCIPLE 8** Keep the experiment protocol as simple as possible (given the research question under consideration).

Having noted this somewhat obvious principle, we need to address some concrete aspects of the protocol. We must decide what is the exact task that our subjects will be performing during the experiment. In other words, what are the precise steps that each experiment treatment will comprise? For example, in the market experiment discussed thus far, we must create a DA environment for the DA treatment. This entails creating the institution, setting the rules of the institution, and being prepared to communicate those rules to the subjects the day of the experiment. Similarly, we must do this for the PO, the E, and the I environments.

Appropriately constructing an experiment in part entails following principles 9–13, described later.

Paper based or computer based?

First we must decide whether the data will be collected using pencil and paper or electronically. In other words, we must decide whether the subjects will record their decisions using sheets of paper or by entering them into a computer-aided device. The decision whether to conduct a paper-based experiment or a computer-based experiment depends on several factors.[16] The primary factor is whether one's subjects can handle a computer. If not, one either has to resort to a paper-based experiment or have assistant experimenters (enumerators) to help participants submit their responses.

If one is dealing with less educated subject populations, as is typically the case in poor rural areas (the usual settings for IFPRI projects, for example), it is usually expected that one will either conduct a paper-based experiment or hire enumerators to help subjects record their responses. The latter approach raises other issues, such as "experimenter" (enumerator) effects other than those arising from the primary experimenter; however, we can typically control such effects ex ante by training enumerators and ensuring that the same enumerators are present across treatments and ex post by including enumerator fixed effects in the analysis. *These effects should not be neglected, because one can lose control over one's experiment in this manner.*

The secondary factor that should be considered when deciding whether to conduct a paper-based or a computer-aided experiment is feasibility. Typically, computer-based experiments proceed faster and can lead to more accurate data collection. However, the computer software needs to be programmed and tested or piloted. This is likely to lead to last-minute changes in the field, which tend to be costly (in terms of time) and stressful. Furthermore, if one is planning to collect data in remote rural areas where power sources are volatile or nonexistent, one needs to be prepared to recharge equipment using other means, such as solar panels, car batteries, and so on. Also, if one wants subjects' decisions to be communicated to each other via the computer software (as is typically the case between buyers and sellers in a market experiment), one needs to be able to set up a local area network (LAN) in the field, for example, by means of a wireless router.[17] Finally, when conducting computer-based experiments, one must keep in mind that the necessary equipment needs to be physically able to

---

[16]We use the term *computer* broadly to include any device that entails electronic data entry. In other words, the term includes tablets, personal digital assistants (PDAs), cellular phones, and any other electronic devices that may be used to collect data.

[17]Thus far, the IFPRI Mobile Experimental Economics Laboratory (IMEEL, http://www.ifpri.org/book-1135/ourwork/program/ifpri-mobile-experimental-economics-laboratory-imeel) has mainly conducted "pencil-and-paper" experiments, but risk experiments have been conducted and general survey data collected using PDAs and tablets. Nonetheless, IMEEL is equipped with hardware such as PDAs, tablets, laptop computers, an access point (to set up a wireless LAN), and solar panels (for recharging) to conduct computer-aided experiments as necessary.

travel. Unless the experiments are part of long-run projects that will have their own in-house equipment, the equipment usually needs to cross international borders. This implies a need to arrange for proper cases, entry and exit (possibly by means of human "escorts"), travel within the destination country, and so on.

In terms of software, there are several packages for PDA-based programs and computer-aided data collection more broadly. Some examples are Blaise (www.blaise.com/), Surveybe (www.surveybe.com/index.php), CSProX (www.serpro.com/), and SatelliteForms (www.satelliteforms.net/). A software package that has been designed specifically for experimental economics tasks, which is also open source, is z-tree (www.iew.uzh.ch/ztree/index.php; Fischbacher 2007). Furthermore, the websites Veconlab (http://veconlab.econ.virginia.edu/admin.htm), Econport (http://econport.org/), and J-markets (http://jmarkets.ssel.caltech .edu/) contain previously programmed experiments that can be conducted over the Internet.

So the ninth principle for conducting an experiment is:

PRINCIPLE 9 Decide whether your experimental environment will be paper based or computer based. The main deciding factors should be (1) whether your subjects, enumerators, or both can handle computer-based tasks and (2) whether it is feasible to have the computer hard- and software deployed in the field.

Instructions and information

Next we must decide what information our subjects will receive during the experiment. This information is typically communicated to subjects as part of the experiment instructions. This is one of the most important aspects of the experiment protocol, and it is also for this reason that experimentalists have developed the "norm" of making their experiment instructions public. Furthermore, during the experiment instructions tend to be read aloud at the session level in order to guarantee that all participants have the same information regarding the experiment. This also helps to reduce skepticism that may be present among participants, such as the belief that experimenters may seek to deceive some participants.

Specifically, we must decide on the following aspects of the experiment instructions: (1) the framing of the experiment task (will it be neutral or loaded?), (2) how much of the purpose of the experiment is to be revealed to subjects (do we conceal or deceive?), and (3) how subjects' understanding of the experiment task is to be tested. We address each of these issues next.

FRAMING

First, there is the issue of framing. Typically we have the option to use "neutral" or "loaded" instructions for the task at hand.[18] Alternatively, people may refer to these as "nonframed" or "framed," respectively. Traditionally, laboratory experiments in economics have been neutrally framed. The primary reason for this approach is to avoid "priming" and "bias." Namely, the more neutral one can keep the framing, the more one can argue that subjects are less informed about the purpose of the experiment. Consequently, one can argue that the condition of dominance is being better achieved because subjects do not try to give the experimenter the result that he desires.

Despite these good rationales for maintaining neutral framing, the issue becomes more subtle when conducting experiments in the field. Typically field participants do not deal well with neutrally framed instructions. Specifically, if the instructions are too far removed from subjects' day-to-day environment ("obscure" in some sense), they will soon ask the experimenter to illustrate by means of a concrete example. If the experimenter then provides such an example, it can be argued that she is now in a world of loaded framing. Accordingly, she needs to maintain consistency by providing the same (or comparable) example(s) in all experiment sessions.

So ex ante we believe it is better to maintain loaded framing when conducting lablike field experiments unless one feels that such framing severely compromises the purpose of the experiment. In the absence of loaded framing, it is important to verify *even more so than usual* that subjects truly understand the task before they make decisions. We elaborate on how this can be done below.

So the tenth principle in conducting an experiment is:

> **PRINCIPLE 10** Decide whether the experiment will maintain neutral or loaded framing. If neutral, make sure to test subjects' understanding more than if framed.

HOW MUCH TO REVEAL: CONCEALMENT OR DECEPTION?

Second, there is the issue of how much information to reveal about the task at hand and the purpose of the experiment. This is crucial because, to achieve the dominance condition, the experimenter wants to avoid subjects'

---

[18]For a more general typology of framing effects, see Levin, Schneider, and Gaeth (1998). Furthermore, for evidence of framing effects, see Ganzach and Karsahi (1995) and Abbink and Hennig-Schmidt (2006), among others.

behaving in a specific manner merely because they think their behavior is the result the experimenter is looking for.

One way to clearly mitigate this issue is to use deception. Deception can be defined as a clear lie. In other words, a protocol that deceives a subject explicitly tells him something that is untrue. For example, suppose we tell subjects in the market experiment that we are trying to measure the speed at which they make their decisions, whereas our true purpose for conducting the experiment is to study the price at which trade takes place. If we do so, this will be considered deception.

Deception has been used in psychology experiments more than in economics experiments. Traditionally it has been the norm in experimental economics *not* to use deception. In fact, deception can be said to be frowned on in experimental economics.

Concealment, on the other hand, is widely used in experimental economics; it can be seen as a "lie of omission" as opposed to a "lie of commission." In other words, as opposed to telling subjects something that is untrue, concealment entails withholding information from one's subjects. In the earlier example, concealment would entail not telling the subject that one's purpose was to study the price at which trade takes place without lying to her.

Practically, all protocols in experimental economics involve concealment of some sort. Most experimental economists avoid deception unless it is absolutely necessary. In case deception is used, the IRB may ask the researcher to "debrief" his subjects by explaining to them why and how he lied after the fact. In such a case, it is important to explain why the protocol required a deliberate lie in order to study the question at hand. Deceptive protocols are usually scrutinized more closely by IRBs, because it may be argued that they place subjects at higher risk. Furthermore, they may also create a sense of distrust between the overall subject pool and the experimenter, which is particularly significant if there will be repeat interactions.[19]

So the eleventh principle in conducting an experiment is:

PRINCIPLE 11 Determine how much information should be concealed from your subjects. Deception should be used only if absolutely necessary, in which case the protocol should be carefully scrutinized by the IRB. Furthermore, the IRB may ask the experimenter to debrief subjects after the experiment is completed.

---

[19] For more on the effects of deception on future interactions between subjects and experimenters, see Jamison, Karlan, and Schechter (2008).

SUBJECT UNDERSTANDING

Third, there is the issue of understanding. This is important because one does not want to elicit purely random decisions unless that is the purpose of the experiment. Subjects' understanding can be evaluated using different measures. One such measure is whether subjects understand how their earnings will be determined. For example, in the market experiment we might check whether subjects understand how to calculate their profits.

In addition, subjects' understanding may be evaluated based on their understanding of the procedures. For example, subjects in the market experiment may be asked what pieces of information will be available to them at a given point in time. Furthermore, they may be asked whether they are allowed to trade after a certain time limit has been exceeded.

Typical laboratory experimenters try to improve subjects' understanding by presenting subjects with quizzes, practice questions, and so on. A similar approach can be adopted in field experiments. One approach that seems to work reasonably well, particularly when conducting paper-based experiments (because one needs to save time), is to do "communal" understanding exercises. For example, when conducting an experiment session, the experimenter may ask questions of the subjects as a group. One caveat to this approach is that the experimenter needs to make sure that everyone is following each question and understands the explanation. Often one or two subjects (such as community or group leaders) tend to want to dominate the discussion. The experimenter should tactfully control this. It is important to repeat the explanation several times, present several different scenarios, and ensure that all subjects have an opportunity to participate in the discussion. This mitigates the possibility that those subjects who are less likely to understand will "fall through the cracks."

The rule I typically apply is comparable to that I use when teaching in the classroom: there are some subjects who understand the procedures the first time around; there is a majority of subjects who understand the procedures only once they have been repeated and supported by means of examples; and finally, there are some subjects who are unlikely to understand even after several examples (these are typically subjects who need more time to digest the new environment and procedures). It is important to try to get these subjects on board; if all else fails, one should make note of those subjects (for example, by annotating their seat numbers) in order to conduct sensitivity analysis ex post: for example, by dropping those observations to see whether the findings are robust. One of the golden rules for gauging understanding is to look at subjects' faces. For example, "dazed looks" are never a good sign; one had better explain the experiment again!

So the twelfth principle in conducting an experiment is:

PRINCIPLE 12 At a minimum, do "communal" exercises to test subjects' understanding. Be wary of those subjects who are likely to fall through the cracks and of dazed looks!

PAYMENT PROTOCOL: SINGLE OR DOUBLE BLIND?

Now we need to address the issue of payment for participation in experiments. Typically it has been the norm in experimental economics to pay subjects for participation in experiments. There are several rationales for doing so. First, like any other persons, (potential) subjects have opportunity costs for their time. If one expects them to spend a few hours making decisions and answering questions, it is only logical to reward them for their time. Second—and this goes back to the basic issues we discussed previously—both salience and dominance dictate that in order to properly align subjects' preferences with the purpose of the experiment, (monetary) rewards or incentives should be administered and satisfy certain conditions. Third, it can be argued that subjects take the task at hand "more seriously" when there are real incentives at stake. Finally, subjects typically really appreciate experimental payments, particularly the rural poor.

Payment for experimental participation gives rise to several complications. The practical implications (that is, in terms of handling large amounts of cash in the field) will be discussed in greater detail in the following section. However, there are other more subtle complications.

One of the main issues is whether to maintain a single- or a double-blind payment protocol. This issue ties into the concept of privacy that was raised previously when discussing the dominance condition. The difference lies in the extent to which other subjects and the experimenter know the treatment (and earnings) of a given subject. The rationale stems from medical experiments in which double-blind protocols have been maintained to mitigate "experimenter bias."

In experimental economics, typically protocols have been single blind in that other subjects do *not* know the treatments (and earnings) of a given subject and vice versa, but the experimenter *does* know such information. All that the experimenter has to ensure in such a circumstance is that the earnings of each subject are kept private from everyone other than the experimenter(s). This protocol is usually fairly easy to implement in the field by (1) separating subjects from their peers during the experiment, (2) introducing envelopes or other devices to "hide" earnings both during and after the experiment, and (3) paying subjects in private and individually. The experimenter can furthermore reiterate as part of her instructions that she will not publicly reveal individual earnings to other subjects at any point during or after the experiment.

However, the experimental literature has also shown that under certain circumstances, double-blind protocols can significantly affect subjects' decisionmaking. This has been shown in "social preference" experiments such as dictator, bargaining, and trust games (see, for example, Hoffman et al. 1994 and Hoffman, McCabe, and Smith 1996). The basic rationale is the following: as we remove subjects' decisionmaking from the "scrutiny" of the experimenter (and of course other subjects), subjects are more likely to reveal their true "colors." Specifically, because social-preference experiments typically involve "moral" decisionmaking (such as whether to equally share an amount of money), decisions made in such environments may be more susceptible to scrutiny by the experimenter.

Although the use of double-blind protocols, particularly in social-preference experiments, may be important, implementing such protocols in the field will typically be complicated for a few reasons. First, a double-blind protocol requires that the experimenter be unable to "identify" the subject. As a result, some laboratory experiments that have maintained a double-blind protocol have used keyed mailboxes to provide payment to subjects—an approach that would be complex to implement in the field given the typical conditions (more on this later). Second, to guarantee a fully double-blind protocol (and thus be unable to identify the subject), the experimenter cannot collect "covariates" (that is, observable characteristics) and link them to the subjects, as is typically done in the field. Given the importance of such covariates in being able to generalize the findings of the experiment (depending on its purpose), it is practically impossible to maintain a strict double-blind protocol.

Camerer (2011) points out that it is not always clear that scrutiny is a major issue in experimental contexts. In addition, it can be argued that a strong focus on privacy and anonymity in the experiment instructions can reduce the external validity of the experiment task by stressing selfish behavior or by making participants overly conscious about the fact that they are under observation. So at the end of the day it must be left to the experimenter's discretion what type of payment protocol he chooses to maintain or implement in the field, particularly for the subject pool under consideration.

So the thirteenth principle in conducting an experiment is:

PRINCIPLE 13 Decide on your payment protocol (single or double blind), and communicate that to your subjects via the instructions so they understand the level of privacy involved in the experiment protocol. It is important to communicate this tactfully in order not to cause paranoia among the subjects.

> **BOX 2.3   Principles for designing an experiment: Experiment protocol**
>
> 1. Obtain the required approval to conduct an experiment by acquiring certification from the Collaborative Institutional Training Initiative (CITI) program and submitting the experiment protocol to an institutional review board (IRB). Also obtain permission from any local authorities or other institutions whose approval is necessary.
>
> 2. When designing the experiment protocol, keep the tasks your subjects are faced with as simple as possible. If necessary, avoid a complicated protocol by creating multiple experiments.
>
> 3. Decide whether your experiment will be paper based or computer based.
>
> 4. Decide whether to present the experiment to subjects using nondescript terms (for example, "type A players," "type B players," "task") that are not drawn from everyday life or using everyday terms ("buyers," "sellers," "market"). The first approach is known as "neutral" or "context-free" framing, the second as "loaded" or "context-specific" framing. If using neutral framing, make an extra effort to test subjects' understanding of the task they will face.
>
> 5. Determine how much information should be concealed from your subjects. Deception should be used only if absolutely necessary, in which case the protocol should be carefully scrutinized by the IRB. The IRB may ask the experimenter to tell subjects the truth after the experiment is completed.
>
> 6. Make sure subjects understand the experiment's rules and what they are supposed to do: repeat explanations or ask subjects questions, as necessary. Be wary of dazed looks!
>
> 7. When paying subjects for their participation, decide whether a given subject's payment will be known to the experimenter but not to the other subjects (single-blind payment protocol) or whether it will be unknown both to the experimenter and to other subjects (double-blind payment protocol). Whichever approach is used, make sure subjects understand it.
>
> **Source:** Author.

We now discuss how to go about implementing the experiment protocol.

IMPLEMENTATION: "IT'S ALL ABOUT THE DETAILS" (CONTINUED)

There are several principles involved in implementing the experiment protocol discussed in the previous section. Full accounts of principles 14–19 are given later, but some of them can be briefly summarized here. First, a sample must be drawn and randomized across experiment treatments and sessions. Second, depending on who is in the sample, the language of the experiment needs to be adjusted. Specifically, typical field experiments in developing countries will take place in a language other than English; accordingly, the experimenter must work closely with local translators if he does not know the participants' primary language. Third, the experimenter must create a "laboratory" in the field. The usual conditions in poor rural areas can make this complex. Fourth, the experimenter must handle large amounts of cash in the field in order to pay subjects. Finally, the experimenter needs to decide how and at what point to collect observable characteristics of the subjects. We discuss each of these issues in further detail in the following sections.

Sampling

Identifying an appropriate population and drawing a sample in the field is not an easy task. One of the major deciding factors as to who makes up the target population stems from the purpose of the research. For example, Grosh and Muñoz (1996) explain that the World Bank Living Standards Measurement Study (LSMS) surveys, which are mainly intended to shed light on determinants of household behavior and to produce a comprehensive monetary measure of welfare and its distribution, are designed to represent the whole population of a country, as well as those of certain subgroups of the population (the "analytical domains").[20]

However, typical research questions addressed at IFPRI, for example, are intended to inform policies on how to alleviate poverty and cut hunger and malnutrition. As a result, the "IFPRI" population is usually narrowed to those who are either in or from poor, typically rural, areas. So, almost by definition, the target population for IFPRI research consists of people in poor areas of developing countries and not necessarily the whole population of any given country. Therefore, contrary to the typical LSMS population, the IFPRI population is not countrywide but rather focused on a specific analytical domain within a country.[21]

This said, the general issues that need to be addressed to properly draw a sample of interest for one's experiment (and one's study more broadly) are common. For the time being, assume that one has identified the

---

[20] Grosh, Margaret; Muñoz, Juan. 1996. *A Manual for Planning and Implementing the Living Standards Measurement Study Survey.* © World Bank. www-wds.worldbank.org/external/default/ WDSContentServer/WDSP/IB/2000/02/24/000009265_3961219093409/Rendered/PDF/multi_ page.pdf. License: Creative Commons Attribution CC BY 3.0.

[21] To some extent, this is a bold statement because IFPRI seeks to study the behavior of the poor, wherever they may be—even if they are in urban or periurban areas. Furthermore, IFPRI may also address research questions targeted at the nonpoor, for example, when studying agribusinesses, large-scale farming practices, and so on.

population of interest and that one actually has access to such a population. The main question is how does one go about drawing a sample from this population; that is, what issues need to be considered? We address this question, to a certain extent, next, drawing largely from Grosh and Muñoz (1996).

The sample design should determine the number and locations of the households to be observed in a way that best achieves the goals of the research within budgetary, organizational, cultural, and political constraints. The following issues must be considered:

1. To reliably depict the overall situation of the target population, the selected sample should contain a sufficient number of households, scattered as much as possible throughout the relevant "analytical domains" (for example, rural areas). However, to reduce the costs, simplify management, and control the quality of the interviews, the sample size and its geographic dispersal must be kept within reasonable limits.

2. The target populations of these analytical domains may contain certain subgroups, such as high- and lowland areas or other aggregates that deserve to be studied separately. The sample of households should adequately represent each of these subgroups as well as the target population as a whole.

3. Each household in the target population should be given a chance to be selected in the sample. To simplify survey design and analysis, this chance should be similar for all households, or at least for all households in the same large domain.

Some insights into how to arbitrate among these objectives and constraints can be obtained from a quick review of four concepts: (1) sampling error, (2) nonsampling error, (3) multistage sampling, and (4) analytical domains.

SAMPLING ERROR

Sampling error is the error inherent in making inferences for a whole population from observing only some of its members. Several good textbooks explore this complex issue (see Annex II of Grosh and Muñoz 1996 as well as the disclaimers pertaining to the references). However, it is important to bear in mind two general conclusions of sampling theory when thinking about sampling error. First, the law of diminishing returns underlies the relationship between sample size and sampling error. Roughly speaking, other things being equal, the sampling error is inversely proportional to the square root of the sample size. This means that, even with the best design, to reduce the error of a particular sample by half, the number of households visited must be quadrupled.

Second, the sample size needed for a given level of precision is almost independent of the total population (for large-enough populations). For instance, a 500-household sample would give essentially the same sampling precision whether it was extracted from a population of 10,000 or 1,000,000 households, or indeed from an infinite population. An intuitive grasp of this seemingly striking statistical fact can be obtained by noticing that, in order to test if a soup is salty enough, an army cook does not need to take a larger sip from the regimental pot.

NONSAMPLING ERROR

Beside sampling errors, data from a household study (survey or experiment) are vulnerable to other inaccuracies stemming from causes as diverse as refusals, respondent fatigue, experimenter or enumerator errors, and the lack of an adequate sample frame. These are collectively known as nonsampling errors. Nonsampling errors are harder to predict and quantify than sampling errors, but it is well accepted that good planning, management, and supervision of field operations are the most effective ways to keep them under control. Moreover, it is likely that management and supervision will be more difficult for larger samples than for smaller ones. Thus one would expect nonsampling errors to increase with sample size.[22]

MULTISTAGE SAMPLING

Third, there is the issue of how to actually do the sampling. Grosh and Muñoz (1996) note that samplers usually do not have a single complete list of households from which to draw a random sample. Even if such a list were available, a sample taken from it would entail high travel costs because selected households would be spread thinly over large areas. Both of these problems can be diminished by using two or more stages in sampling.

In the version of two-stage sampling generally used for LSMS surveys, a certain number of small area units are selected with probability proportional to size, and then a fixed number of households are taken from each selected area, giving each household in the area the same chance of being chosen. The area units are usually the smallest recognizable geographic

[22]Grosh, Margaret; Muñoz, Juan. 1996. *A Manual for Planning and Implementing the Living Standards Measurement Study Survey.* © World Bank. www-wds.worldbank.org/external/default/ WDSContentServer/WDSP/IB/2000/02/24/000009265_3961219093409/Rendered/PDF/multi_ page.pdf. License: Creative Commons Attribution CC BY 3.0.

units in the national census. These are usually census enumeration areas, which are aggregates of 50–200 households. These may be called primary sampling units (PSUs). To accommodate this procedure, it is necessary to have a listing of all households per PSU.

The two-stage procedure just described has several advantages. It provides an approximately self-weighted sample (that is, each household has roughly the same chance of being selected), which simplifies analysis. It also reduces the travel time of the field teams relative to a single-stage sample, because the households to be visited are clumped together in the PSUs rather than spread out evenly over the whole country. An additional advantage of selecting a fixed number of households in each PSU at the second stage is that this makes it easy to distribute the workload among field teams.

A two-stage sample, however, will yield larger errors than a simple random sample with the same number of households because neighboring households tend to have similar characteristics. A sample of households drawn in two stages will therefore reflect less of a population's diversity than a simple random sample of the same size. The influence of two-stage sampling on the precision of the estimates is called the *cluster effect*. As would be expected, the cluster effect grows with the number of households selected in each PSU. In other words, for a fixed-total sample size, a design with more PSUs and fewer households in each PSU will provide more precise estimates of sample statistics than a design with fewer PSUs and more households in each PSU.

Implementation of the sample begins with the sample frame—the complete list or file of units from which the sample units are selected. To develop a sample frame from census data, it is important to obtain a computer-readable list of all PSUs, along with a measure of size, such as the number of households, the number of dwellings, or the population, recorded for each of them. After all the data have been entered, checks should be carried out to ensure that no PSUs have been omitted from the listing and that all the data are correct. After the sample frame has been reviewed, the actual selection of the sample of PSUs to be visited by the survey team can proceed.[23] Grosh and Muñoz discuss in detail how one can go about this, and the reader is referred to their text for further discussion.

Suffice it to say that once we have the sample of PSUs established, we can proceed to the second stage of the sampling. Grosh and Muñoz (1996) note that a list of all dwellings in each selected PSU is needed to determine which dwellings on the list will participate in the study. Usually this list

---

[23]Ibid.

will have to be created or updated for the survey, though in some cases it can be borrowed from a census or from another survey. The option of borrowing an existing list should be examined critically, however, to ensure that the existing lists are recent and complete and have good addresses or GPS coordinates. In particular, demographic mobility makes it dangerous to use lists that will be more than one or two years old by the time of the actual fieldwork. The information on the list should make it easy to locate the households once they are selected. Typically, in rural areas a good street address system will be nonexistent, so references to GPS coordinates supported by references to landmarks with names, nicknames, and cell phone numbers of the household head, other household members, and possibly neighbors should be reported.[24]

ANALYTICAL DOMAINS

As mentioned previously, for policy or mandate reasons some subgroups of the population are so important that the study is expected to provide separate, reliable results for them. This is usually the case for IFPRI studies, whose primary focus is the (rural) poor. Typical examples include division of subgroups into urban and rural locations and into major administrative units such as states or regions. The design will then have to ensure a minimum sample size within each of these subgroups, which can then be called analytical domains.

Grosh and Muñoz (1996) note that for large domains this may occur automatically, whereas in other cases it may be necessary to oversample certain analytical domains and to modify the expansion factors (also called "sampling weights") accordingly. The two-stage sampling procedure is applied independently within each of those differently weighted domains. Analysts would often also like to have sufficient sample sizes in smaller analytical groups. This ideal, however, cannot be fully achieved for all possible analytical domains because it would result in a prohibitively large total sample. Therefore, defining the most significant partitions of a sample entails establishing some priorities at the design stage. Often these will be dictated not only by policy relevance but also by local statistical folklore, geopolitical considerations, and the constraints raised previously.[25]

SAMPLING FOR EXPERIMENTAL IMPACT ASSESSMENTS

The procedures for drawing a sample for a randomized experiment—this includes lablike field experiments in which some part of the sample

---

[24]Ibid.
[25]Ibid.

is randomly allocated to one treatment and the other part to (an)other treatment(s)—are similar to those described earlier for a general study. Generally we use a two-stage approach, which is described by Himelein (2011): first we assign PSUs to treatment and control groups (or alternatively two or more treatment groups). Then we select units of analysis (such as households) within the selected PSUs according to the listing procedures discussed previously.

Once we have our sampling frame, the number of PSUs, and the number of units of analysis in each PSU, we can perform power calculations. Specifically, we can calculate the sample size we will need to credibly identify a minimum detectable effect for our treatment(s).[26] Researchers can use the "sampsi" routine in Stata to do such power calculations.[27] It is useful to know the formula upon which this is based. According to Himelein (2011), the formula is as follows:

$$N = \left[4\sigma^2 \left(z_{\alpha/2} + z_{\beta} \right)^2 / D^2 \right] \left[1 + \rho(H - 1) \right], \qquad (2.1)$$

where σ^2 is the variance in the population outcome metric (basically, the range of differences you expect in the outcome variable, which is usually best calculated using previous data: for example, from a previously conducted household survey); D is the effect size (basically, how much of an impact your treatment will have—notice the trade-off between effect size and sample size); z-scores are from a standard normal cumulative distribution where the critical values α and β are related to "type I" and "type II" errors, respectively (basically, type I error is the probability that the null hypothesis is rejected although it is in fact true, also referred to as a "false positive," and type II error is the probability that the null hypothesis is not rejected when it is in fact false, also referred to as a "false negative"—lower type I and type II error both require larger sample sizes); and the last factor relates to how many clusters and households we select into our sample (specifically, ρ is the intracluster correlation effect, a measure of how similar observations within each PSU tend to be, and H is the number of observations in each cluster—the more similar households are to each other and the more households we have in each cluster, the larger will be the overall sample size needed).

Beyond the standard issues discussed previously, there are typically additional things to consider depending on our experimental design—for

---

[26] The World Bank: The World Bank authorizes the use of this material subject to the terms and conditions on its website, www.worldbank.org/terms.

[27] Another useful resource is the optimal design software discussed by Spybrook et al. (2011).

example, if we decide to stratify the sample by partitioning it to ensure a sufficient number of observations in all categories, if we decide to oversample by taking a larger proportion of observations in certain strata than in the overall target population, or if we design the experiment to have more than two treatments, in which case the required sample size will increase very quickly. Finally, as mentioned previously, the sampsi routine assumes normality. So, to the extent that the distribution of outcome responses (upon which the effect will be tested) is not expected to conform to normality, the researcher should take this into account when performing power calculations.[28]

For an additional discussion on sample size and power, specifically in the context of randomized experimental designs, the reader is referred to Duflo, Glennerster, and Kremer (2007).

So the fourteenth principle in conducting an experiment is:

PRINCIPLE 14 Identify a target population, and draw a sample according to a multistage procedure, taking into account sampling and nonsampling errors as well as analytical domains. Make sure that the sample size is based on careful "calculations" according to equation 2.1 or, alternatively, using Stata's "sampsi" routine. Bear in mind the directional relationships between sample size (SS) and the following components: variance (+, lower variance → lower SS), effect size (−, bigger effect size → lower SS), number of clusters (−, more clusters → lower SS), confidence (+, more confidence → higher SS), power (+, more power → higher SS), similarity of clusters (+, more similarity → higher SS), and observations per cluster (+, more observations per cluster → higher SS). These relationships are typically nonlinear. Also, keep in mind that "sampsi" assumes normality.

RECRUITMENT

Once we have drawn a sample according to the procedures in the previous section, we need to actually invite the selected participants for the study. Our main goal during the recruitment stage is to inform subjects about the study sufficiently to ensure that those who have been selected actually participate. So in the recruitment phase the experimenter and his assistants (enumerators) face a tension between informing selected subjects about the study sufficiently that they feel compelled to participate and priming them too much about the purpose of the study. Nonetheless, getting as many of the selected subjects as possible to attend is of primary importance in order to mitigate attrition, which can be problematic (we return to attrition later).

---

[28] The World Bank: The World Bank authorizes the use of this material subject to the terms and conditions on its website, www.worldbank.org/terms.

The first issue that needs to be addressed is how much information to reveal to selected participants about the study when inviting them to attend. Specifically, we want to reveal some information about the experiment (as an informative "teaser"), but not too much. Furthermore, we typically want to provide all subjects with the same information at this stage, regardless of their treatment status. So the typical invitation to attend an experiment contains (1) the date, time, and place of the study; (2) a brief and general statement of the purpose of the study (that is, a rough idea of what the study will be about, for example, the main topic, such as "market decisionmaking," "insurance," or "remittances"); (3) what will be expected of the participant (that is, that the subject will have to make decisions and answer questions); and (4) what type of compensation can be expected (that is, typically a fixed show-up payment of X and additional average earnings of Y depending on the decisions made during the study; sometimes IRBs will also require revelation of minimum and maximum earnings).

In some instances, the invitation may actually be formulated as a formal letter in order to appear more professional. These letters tend to be a great tool for ensuring higher participation. A formal letter endorsed by, for example, the local government or a well-known nongovernmental organization is typically more convincing than a "blank" invitation, so it is likely to reduce attrition. Sometimes the invitation is provided orally by the recruiters. This depends on (1) what is appropriate based on the cultural norms under consideration and (2) the relationship between the recruiters and potential participants. For example, in some cases the experimenter may use recruiters from the local census bureau or extension office. These individuals will typically be familiar to the potential participants. Accordingly, the participants may already trust them, and a formal letter may be unnecessary. In some cases, the experimenter may also choose to obtain the consent of subjects—via the recruiters—at this stage as opposed to on the day of the experiment.

An important aspect to keep in mind is that, depending on what type of information we provide or how such information is framed, we have different types of people selecting to participate in the study. For example, if we frame experimental earnings as being risky, risk-seeking subjects might become more likely to participate in the study. So we should be careful with how the invitation is framed. This form of selection can pose a threat to both the internal and the external validity of the study. It does not necessarily threaten internal validity as long as participants select similarly into the experiment treatments. However, even if they do, external validity may still be compromised. So it is important that we get (almost) everyone who was drawn for the experiment sample to participate in order to guarantee that our treatment estimates are at least representative of the target population identified in principle 14.

The second issue that needs to be addressed at this stage concerns the types of incentives that selected participants can be provided to show up as invited. Two such incentives were already mentioned previously, namely the show-up payment (this is typically intended to cover subjects' transportation costs) and the additional earnings (these are typically intended to achieve salience and dominance and, at the same time, reward subjects for the opportunity cost of their time). However, there may be other ways of providing incentives or reducing subjects' transportation costs and thus facilitating their participation.

For example, suppose that the lablike field experiments were part of a larger study that would also entail RCTs and suppose that the randomization for participation in the latter experiments were publicly conducted upon conclusion of the lablike field experiments. This would provide additional incentives for selected participants to attend these experiments. Furthermore, suppose that the experimenter decided to provide transportation from a central location (for example, the center of each village) to the location of the experiment (the laboratory); we might expect this to increase participation in the experiment.

The third issue that needs to be addressed is whom within a household to invite for participation in the experiment. Technically, this is an issue that should already have been addressed at the sampling stage; it will just need to be implemented at the recruitment stage. However, we raise it explicitly here because the experimenter needs to make sure that her recruiters are clear on the protocol as to whom to invite and how to deal with nonresponse or with other people who may be interested. For example, suppose that the experimenter is interested only in heads of households. In such a case, recruiters need to make sure to clarify this to the households and ensure that heads of households are properly informed about the date, time, and place of the study. Also, they need to be informed how to deal with nonresponse: that is, heads of households who report upon invitation that they will not be able to make it.

Finally, we must decide whom to choose as recruiters and must train them appropriately. It is important that recruiters be trained collectively, because decentralized training can lead to confusion and thus lead to complications during the experiment sessions. A suggested strategy is to inform recruiters just sufficiently about the study. This will mitigate the possibility that they will provide subjects with too much information ex ante. For example, although the recruiters need to know which participants are supposed to show up at what time and that there are different show-up times, it is typically not necessary for them to know that these times are associated with different treatments. So use caution in what information is provided.

So the fifteenth principle in conducting an experiment is:

PRINCIPLE 15 Formulate a proper recruitment strategy to ensure maximum attendance. This entails having a proper invitation (possibly in the form of an official letter supported by an additional letter from a "trusted" party) that provides necessary, relevant information that entices subjects to attend the experiment. Make sure all recruiters are trained collectively and are aware of the proper protocol for recruitment (that is, what information to provide, whether to obtain the consent of the subjects, how to deal with nonresponses, and so on).

Collaborators: Translators, assistants, and beyond

When conducting experiments, particularly lablike field experiments in developing countries, the experimenter is likely to need different types of assistants.

First, the experimenter needs recruiters for different purposes. One of the primary tasks is to list subjects during the listing phase of the sampling stage. At this stage, the recruiter's task is to go to the PSUs defined by the experimenter (sampler) and list all of the households. A secondary task of the recruiters is to actually recruit selected participants for the study. It should be left to the experimenter's discretion whether the same recruiters are used for these two tasks. To the extent that they are or that one set of recruiters is a subset of the other, the experimenter should be careful at what stages she reveals what types of information about the study to the recruiters. Also, there seems to be evidence of "Hawthorne effects" in repeat interactions between subjects and enumerators ("recruiters"; see, for example, Zwane et al. 2011).[29] So this should be kept in mind when assessing whether to use the same recruiters for different stages.

Second, during the experiment the experimenter will typically need several types of assistance depending on how he chooses to conduct his experiment. The main issue that usually needs to be addressed is language, because the primary researcher—who is usually the main experimenter—may not speak the national or local language in question. Facing this

---

[29]A Hawthorne effect occurs when subjects modify an aspect of their behavior simply in response to the fact that they know they are being studied, not in response to any particular experimental manipulation.

constraint, there are typically two ways of proceeding with the experiment. Although both approaches require close interaction with a translator, they are fairly different in terms of how one ends up conducting the experiment.

In the first approach, the main experimenter conducts the experiment sessions herself; however, she has someone interpret what she says in a line-by-line manner. In the second approach, the main experimenter trains the translator extensively on the protocol to ensure that he understands it and then leaves the experiment sessions up to this person. There are pros and cons to either approach. Although the first approach enables the main experimenter to maintain great control over the experiment session, line-by-line translation could be argued to appear mechanical. On the other hand, although the second approach is more natural, the main experimenter is no longer seen by the subjects as "the experimenter" but is seen as having "passed the torch" to the translator. So one could argue that control by the primary experimenter has been reduced considerably.

I have typically either conducted my own experiment sessions (when those could be conducted in languages that I could speak) or, if not, I have opted for the first approach. My main reason for this was to maintain experimenter control in a manner that is comparable to the standards of typical laboratory experiments in Western societies. In addition to using line-by-line translation, I usually train the translator prior to the experiment sessions, although perhaps not as much as I would if I were using the second approach. I have found that being able to observe subjects' facial expressions during the experiment, as is the case in the first approach, is usually extremely useful in gauging understanding despite the language barrier.

In addition to a translator, the experimenter will typically need assistants to help him perform the procedures required by the experiment. In paper-based experiments, he will usually need an assistant to record or verify subjects' decisions and calculate earnings "behind the scenes" (in computer-based experiments, this task will typically be performed by a server). This task is of crucial importance to ensure successful data collection. So it is important to assign it to someone one trusts. For example, this could be the main experimenter's colleague or coauthor, or, in absence thereof, the task could be assigned to a lead enumerator to whom what needs to be done has been carefully explained. It is likely that the experimenter will also need assistance in the "laboratory" for numerous purposes, such as handing out forms and envelopes and assisting illiterate subjects to complete forms or make sure they understand the procedures.

Finally, the experimenter will likely need a field coordinator. This person is typically in charge of all the logistical details on the day of the experiment. She ensures that subjects show up the day of the experiment as necessary, at the required place and time. This person could also be the person who is in charge of the listing and recruitment stages described previously. If the experimenter plans to conduct a postexperiment survey directly following the experiment, it will also be necessary to make sure trained enumerators are present after the experiment to conduct the surveys. We return to this issue when discussing issues related to surveys.

So the sixteenth principle in conducting an experiment is:

> **PRINCIPLE 16** Hire a team of collaborators that comprises a field coordinator (who coordinates the listing, recruitment, and show-up of participants at the experiment), a main translator (who will either do line-by-line translation or conduct the experiment herself), and if necessary an assistant experimenter (who will perform the necessary calculations behind the scenes, provided the experiment is paper based), additional assistants (who will facilitate the procedures of the experiment), and enumerators (who will conduct any necessary surveys). It is important for you to be convinced that your team of collaborators is well equipped to perform the tasks at hand.

Creating a lab in the field

Creating a "laboratory" in the field can be a daunting task, especially when the experiments are to be conducted in a rural area of a developing country. To create an experimental laboratory we need a large locale with 20–40 tables and chairs, with some type of dividers to mitigate peer effects. Preferably, the locale will also have a large board in the front of the room to use in explaining the experimental task.

Given these requirements, the typical candidate for a laboratory in the field is a classroom in the village school. Alternatively, it could be a meeting room at the main gathering place of a farmers' group or association. More generally, it could also be a rented locale in a neighboring town, such as a meeting or event room in the town hotel. The choice of locale mainly depends on availability, as well as budgetary and time constraints. Given a sufficiently large budget, one can almost always transport participants to a locale that satisfies these criteria; however, transportation costs (in terms of actual costs and opportunity costs of time) then become an issue.

Consider the case of a classroom in the village school. The benefit of setting up one's laboratory at such a venue is that it will typically be easily accessible by the subjects in the village. The lower the transportation costs to get to the experiment, the higher the likelihood that subjects will show up for the experiment as instructed. This said, there are a few drawbacks to using such a locale as one's laboratory.

First, although a classroom may be available, school may be in session. As a result, one should be prepared for an "audience" of children and possibly schoolteachers with all the associated distractions that emerge. Second, in poorer rural areas, classrooms can be relatively underdeveloped. Specifically, they may be small, with a limited number of tables and chairs. Thus they may not be ideal for a laboratory. In some instances, the school library—if not occupied—can function as a better locale. Third, it is likely that one's subjects will come from different villages. Therefore, to minimize transportation costs for the majority of the subjects, one has to select the school that is most centrally located vis-à-vis the villages in question, unless one is willing to change locales across villages. This is certainly possible; however, one should be prepared to set up the laboratory every time one switches classrooms. So this should be factored into one's travel time and so on. Furthermore, the rooms should be set up in a comparable manner for each session to avoid unnecessary differences across sessions. Obviously, one can control for this ex post (for example, by controlling for participants' seating and approximate distances between them); however, avoiding such issues by design is "cleaner."

You might also consider an alternative venue, such as the meeting place of a farmers' association or an event room at a hotel in the nearest town. Both these venues are more likely to be better developed, with proper tables, chairs, and a board. Also, they are more likely to be larger rooms that can accommodate a greater number of people. Finally, it is likely that one can control audience and crowding effects more easily at such venues, because they are likely to be less crowded with interested audiences. However, these venues also have their drawbacks.

First, they are likely to cost more, although this is unlikely to be one's most major concern in this case. Second, and more important, they are more likely to be farther away from subjects. This is of concern because it increases the transportation cost to subjects, and that increases the likelihood of attrition. We should be highly concerned about this. One approach that I have applied but that depends on one's budget is to organize transportation from central village locations to the experiment site. This enables the experimenter to find a locale that is "ideal" in some sense.

Beyond the issues previously discussed, creation of a laboratory in the field also entails other things. For example, depending on the protocol in question, it may be useful to have an adjacent room where the primary assistant experimenter can sit and record decisions "behind the scenes." This is also where the money can be handled (see more later). In the absence thereof, it is ideal to have a "laboratory" that is large enough that the assistant experimenter can be seated at the back of the room, somewhat unbeknownst to subjects.

Finally, to mitigate peer effects it is useful to be able to separate subjects from each other as much as possible. In addition, it is useful to introduce dividers once subjects are going to make decisions. In university laboratories, dividers tend to be standard fixtures. In field laboratories, one can use anything from voting boxes to large, sturdy pieces of carton to actual boxes. Sometimes subjects may find this use of dividers strange, so my experience has been to motivate them to see these as "houses." The typical analogy drawn is with the decisions that are taken in one's home behind closed doors. Figures 2.1 and Figure 2.2 show sample locales of IFPRI experiments.

So the seventeenth principle in conducting an experiment is:

PRINCIPLE 17 Secure an "ideal" locale (that is, a spacious one with tables, chairs, and a board, and relatively easily accessible) to serve as the laboratory for your experiment. Make sure the assistant experimenter has a private area or room in which to perform his tasks during the experiment. Buy dividers locally if possible; these could vary from voting boxes to sturdy cartons to standard boxes.

FIGURE 2.1   Experiment session in Ethiopia

Source: Hill, R. V., and A. Viceisza. 2012. "A Field Experiment on the Impact of Weather Shocks and Insurance on Risky Investment." *Experimental Economics* 15 (2): 341–371. http://dx.doi.org/10.1007/s10683-011-9303-7. © The authors 2011. Reprinted with permission.

FIGURE 2.2 Experiment session in Vietnam

Source: Torero and Viceisza (2011).

(Don't) show me the money

As alluded to previously, economics experiments typically pay subjects in cash for their participation. As a result, the experimenter and the assistant experimenter must handle substantial amounts of cash during the stages of the experiment. Depending on the level of payoffs, a lot of change (that is, money in small denominations) may be necessary. The experimenter should not underestimate the nuisances that typically emerge.

First, because local banks are unlikely to have large amounts of change available at one time, the experimenter should be ready to try multiple banks, make multiple attempts, or seek out other venues that may carry change. For example, in some countries bus drivers will carry lots of change. Second, although it is always an option to get change "bit by bit," it is important to factor in special days such as weekends and holidays. If some of the experiment sessions will take place on weekends, for example, which is likely, the experimenter should plan to have sufficient change to last through the weekend. If all else fails, one can always pay subjects larger amounts and ask for change from them; however, it is best to avoid such situations. Third, large amounts of cash in the field are heavy. Have a proper bag or case *that does not draw too much attention* in which to carry them. Fourth, whenever there is cash involved, there are potential security concerns. When potential participants hear that there are "outsiders paying villagers," everyone will want to know what is going on and perhaps even participate. So the experimenter should be prepared to handle such situations (we return to tactfulness later). The important thing here is to make sure that the "sordid topic of coin" is handled as privately as possible.

Furthermore, the experimenter should always prepare for the worst case and concern herself about the security of the cash. Although I have never had any negative experiences, there are areas where security is of concern. Word of "substantial" amounts of cash could attract those with bad intentions. So try not to handle cash publicly. This is also why it is ideal if the assistant experimenter can be hidden from subjects in the experiment as well as any third-party observers in a separate room or behind a divider at the back of the main experiment room.

On a final note, typically there will be additional assistants present during the experiment (both outside and inside the laboratory). There is safety in numbers, especially if there are some bodyguardlike assistants or enumerators among them. However, if the experimenter deems it necessary to have additional (perhaps even trained security or law enforcement) help, he should always arrange accordingly. This was the case during the remittance experiments reported by Torero and Viceisza (2012).

So the eighteenth principle in conducting an experiment is:

PRINCIPLE 18 Have money available to pay your subjects after the experiments. Take appropriate measures to ensure the security of the field team (in relation to the money). Try not to publicly display cash. Use tact in dealing with cash; be prepared for potential crowds as word travels. Train the field team on how to deal with such potential situations as well.

Surveys: Collecting additional characteristics

Thus far, most of our discussion has focused on experimental data collection. However, there is good reason to spend some time on survey data collection.

First, there are similarities between collecting experimental data and collecting survey data. For example, our previous discussion on sampling, adopted largely from Grosh and Muñoz (1996), was primarily written for survey data, but because the resulting principle 14 derives from sampling theory, it also applies more generally to other types of data collection, such as the collection of experimental data. Also, from an organizational standpoint the two forms of data collection are similar.

Second, collection of experimental data is well suited to certain purposes or types of data, whereas other types of data are better collected using a survey-based approach.[30] For example, suppose we want to collect data on

---

[30] The main differences between the two approaches are that experimental data are (1) revealed preference data as opposed to stated preference data (that is, the experimenter observes actual decisionmaking by subjects as opposed to what they "state" they would do or have done) and (2) collected using an incentive-compatible mechanism that realizes the conditions of monotonicity, salience, and dominance described previously (that is, for all practical purposes, experimental data are collected according to a salient payment procedure).

household income, expenditures, and assets; day-to-day activities on and off the farm; and participation in community organizations, social activities, and social networks. It is easier or more efficient to collect such data using a survey-based approach.

Third, survey data are a complement to experimental data, particularly when conducting field experiments. The typical laboratory experiment collects survey data ex post; however, because of the homogeneity of the subject pool (usually undergraduate students), not much is gained from collecting extensive demographic information. So such surveys are mainly directed toward verifying subjects' understanding of the protocol. In field studies, however, there is much to be gained from collecting demographic data among others. Not only can these data help the experimenter get a sense of the internal validity of the experimental estimates ex post but they can also help him to generalize the findings of the experiment, thus addressing issues related to external validity. We return to this issue when we discuss how to draw inferences from experimental findings.

Fourth, certain types of lablike field experiments have also been embedded in surveys because (1) the protocols allow for it and (2) data collection can proceed faster for a given sample size.[31] Two main issues need to be addressed prior to implementation if one wants to adopt such an approach: (1) potential confounding experimenter effects and (2) whether experiment payments should be hypothetical versus real. Neither issue is unique to the fact that the experiments are being embedded in surveys; however, it tends to be trickier to deal with these issues in this context.[32]

Consider experimenter effects. In a typical experiment, there is one experimenter who is held fixed throughout different sessions, and participants make choices after having been instructed by one such experimenter. When the experiment is embedded in a survey, there is typically more than one experimenter because the enumerators are now the experimenters. Because enumerators' main goal is to complete as many surveys as possible, they may not have the incentives to properly understand the experiments, to properly execute them, or to do either. For example, they may try

---

[31] What I have in mind are cases in which experiment protocols (such as risk experiments or implemented games) are included as modules of a survey. This is different from "survey experiments" (for example, Beegle et al. 2010 and Caeyers, Chalmers, and de Weerd 2012), which seek to experiment with survey design or framing. For a symposium on survey experiments, see the following link: http://psr.iq.harvard.edu/event/psr-conference-survey-experiments. Some examples of experiments that have been embedded in surveys include (1) risk and time preference experiments (see, for example Andersen et al. 2008; Giné et al. 2011; and many IFPRI surveys, some of which are reported by Hill and Viceisza 2012 and Hill, Maruyama, and Viceisza 2012) and (2) dictator game experiments (see, for example, Hill, Maruyama, and Viceisza 2012).

[32] These issues are of even greater importance if the experimental measure to be collected as part of the survey is the primary outcome variable of interest (as opposed to a measure that will be used as a covariate in the analysis).

to "cheat" by manipulating the randomization device if this makes their lives easier. They might also attempt such manipulation to foster relationships between themselves and any participants whom they already know from prior interactions. So when embedding experiments in surveys it is important to (1) a priori train enumerators heavily in the procedures for conducting the experiment (it is important to stress during training that although it is important for subjects to understand the procedures, the enumerators should not "prime" or influence decisionmaking, because enumerators often feel that if a subject does not know an answer or answers incorrectly, they have somehow failed), (2) build checks into the implementation of the experiments so that one can detect whether any "cheating" has occurred, and (3) control ex post for enumerator fixed effects (that is, one must design the collection process so that one can exploit variation across enumerators, villages, and so on to detect any type of strange "clustering").

Next one must consider monetary incentives. There is evidence to suggest that hypothetical and real incentives in experiments can lead to different responses in certain contexts (see Laury and Holt 2008 for lottery choices and Harrison and Rutström 2008 for value elicitation methods more broadly). As a result, whenever we conduct an experiment the question emerges whether to pay for the decisions made within that setup. *Why is this question more important when dealing with experiments in surveys?*

Payment for experiments embedded in surveys is more difficult to implement. Consider the case in which one has 8–12 enumerators, each of which is going to one or two households in one or two villages per day. These enumerators are typically carrying either several copies of paper-based surveys or a PDA or tablet, with the usual supplies such as pens, pencils, notebooks, and calculators. All things considered, hypothetical payments become more attractive in this context, because payoff calibrations will often require small denominations of the local currency. Furthermore, real earnings will require additional bookkeeping at the enumerator and supervisor levels, as well as additional security measures at the centralized level, because the overall cash involved can be substantial for a survey comprising a sufficiently large number of households.

The complexity of implementing real payments may also be exacerbated by the type of experiment in question. Consider, for example, a typical time-preference experiment in which the subject chooses between two amounts of money to be paid one month from now versus seven months from now. In this front-end delay framework, everyone needs to be paid in the future, which implies returning to these households and actually paying them according to their choices. Contrary to the developed-country field, where one may be able to make payments through checks in the mail, the developing-country field may require actually revisiting households if they are sufficiently rural (although there may be more sophisticated measures, such as payments made by cell phones or remittance carriers such as Western Union).

In short, experiments can and have been embedded in surveys; however, the researcher must carefully consider the potential benefits and costs of such an approach. Two types of surveys are typically conducted to complement experimental data. The first type of survey is a postexperiment survey. This type of survey is mainly intended for the following purposes:

1. To collect data that can be used to test subjects' understanding of the experimental procedures.

2. To collect observable characteristics of the participants.

3. To get a better understanding of how subjects perceived the experimental task. This is an important issue that should not be ignored. Often the experimenter may be very clear on her experimental design and protocol and what they are intended to capture. Consequently, she may feel that she has identified the key issues at play. However, the subject may perceive the protocol much differently. If so, there emerges a mismatch between the true data-generating process (DGP) and the experimenter's *perceived* DGP. In terms of later analysis, this will lead to a misspecified model. So it is important for the experimenter to use the postexperiment survey as an opportunity to get a solid understanding of the intuition and rationale that underlie subjects' decisionmaking. For example, in the remittance experiments reported by Torero and Viceisza (2012), subjects were asked to explain the rationale for their decisionmaking after having completed the experimental task. This was part of the postexperiment phase of the experiment session.

The second type of survey is the standard household survey. Its purpose is different from that of the postexperiment survey, because it is intended to capture a broad class of relevant observable characteristics that can be used in ex post analysis. As a result, it is usually much longer than the postexperiment survey.

Two main references on survey design and survey data analysis are Deaton (1995), which mainly addresses econometric issues associated with survey data, and Grosh and Glewwe (2000), which—among other things—discusses the types of modules that are included in typical LSMS household, community, and price data surveys.[33] Typical modules include

---

[33] Some examples of surveys that have been conducted by IFPRI over the years can be found at www.ifpri.org/datasets/results/taxonomy%3A5168.

(1) basic household and demographic information (including a household roster); (2) income, expenditures, or both; (3) assets; (4) production inputs and technologies; (5) production outputs and market access; (6) social networks, participation, and information; (7) perceptions of welfare and shocks; (8) preferences for and beliefs or perceptions about risk (for example, lottery choices), time, trust, cooperation, altruism (for example, dictator games), and coordination; (9) anthropometric measures; and (10) identifier variables, including GPS coordinates. Although this list of modules is by no means exhaustive, it gives a sense of the types of data that are collected by means of household surveys. As is the case for experimental data, modules may be added, subtracted, or substituted depending on the research purpose of the survey as well as the purposes of the complementary experiments.

Now for some concluding remarks on survey design and implementation:

1. Typically each household in the experiment sample will complete a household survey in addition to the postexperiment survey, which is completed by the member of the household who attends the experiment. For a sufficiently long survey, this implies that survey data collection will take much longer than experimental data collection. So a proper sequencing of data collection needs to be arranged with the field coordinator. This is particularly relevant if the experimenter expects that completion of the household survey will affect behavior in the lablike field experiment. This could be due to different types of experimenter effects; for instance, the survey could expose the subject to concepts that will be addressed in the lablike field experiments (see, for example, Zwane et al. 2011 for the case of surveys vis-à-vis an RCT). This issue may be of particular concern when questions in the survey and tasks in the lablike field experiments are framed similarly. In such a case, the experimenter should sequence experimental and survey data collections in such a manner that order or learning effects can be rigorously assessed.

2. It is important that the experimenter train his enumerators carefully on any survey that needs to be conducted, just as he does for the purposes of listing, recruitment, assistance during the experiment, and any other task. For the postexperiment survey, this should be fairly easy (because it tends to be shorter and simpler); however, for the household survey this will be more involved. Typically it is best that enumerators be trained collectively in order to avoid misunderstanding. However, when enumerators are deployed it may be best to have teams of four or five enumerators who in turn report to a lead

enumerator, who in turn reports to the field coordinator, who in turn reports to you.

So the nineteenth principle in conducting an experiment is:

PRINCIPLE 19 Design and conduct surveys to complement your experimental data. Typically, these surveys will be of two types: (1) a relatively short postexperiment survey of 30 to 60 minutes intended to test subjects' understanding, gain a better understanding of their rationale for decision-making, and collect specific individual-level characteristics that may not be collected as part of the household survey and (2) an extensive household survey intended to collect observable characteristics of the household as a whole (to be used to capture heterogeneity across the subject pool). Train enumerators collectively, and make sure that each enumerator reports to a lead enumerator, who in turn reports to the field coordinator, who in turn reports to you.

OTHER PRACTICAL SUGGESTIONS

This section offers some practical suggestions that one should consider when conducting lablike field experiments.

1. **Conduct a pilot experiment.** Pilot experiments are very informative and shed light on many complications that may arise during the actual experiment. A pilot should be taken just as seriously as an actual experiment session. When conducting experiments in rural areas in developing countries, pilots can be a costly affair if one has to travel to the country. So one suggestion is to lump the pilot with travel for other purposes. For example, if one has to travel to the country to plan RCTs or meet with stakeholders for other purposes (such as project updates), this would be a good time to conduct some pilot sessions. It is best not to schedule the pilot too closely to the actual experiments in case substantial changes need to be made to the protocol. This comment applies particularly in the case of a computer-aided experiment, for example, if software changes need to be made.

2. **Plan for attrition.** One way to try to deal with attrition ex ante is to recruit "regular" and "alternate" participants. Alternate participants can usually fill the void for regular participants who do not show up for the experiment. The neatness of this approach is that both regulars and alternates can be randomized into such roles within a given treatment ex ante so that one could argue that these groups

---

BOX 2.4   Principles for designing an experiment: Implementation

1. Identify a target population, and draw an appropriate sample from it. For example, make sure that the sample is large enough and that different population subgroups are sufficiently well represented within it that you can draw valid inferences from it. Also compensate for problems such as errors resulting from the way in which the study is conducted.

2. Develop a recruitment strategy to ensure maximum attendance. This can include sending an official letter or other invitation that provides information and incentives to participate. Make sure all recruiters are trained in such tasks as giving subjects appropriate information about the experiment and getting their consent to participate.

3. Hire a team of collaborators to conduct or assist in conducting the experiment. The team should include a field coordinator who organizes the subjects and a translator, and it may include other assistants as necessary.

4. Secure a spacious, relatively accessible locale with tables, chairs, and a means of instruction (a blackboard, for example) to serve as the laboratory. If the experiment is paper based, make sure the team member who will perform calculations has a private area or room in which to do this work during the experiment.

5. Have money available to pay your subjects after the experiments. Take appropriate measures to ensure the security of the money and convenience in distributing it.

6. Design and conduct surveys to complement the experiment's results. These surveys will typically be (1) a short postexperiment study of subjects' understanding of the experiment, the reasons for their decisions, and their individual characteristics and (2) an extensive study of subjects' households.

Source: Author.

---

are similar across unobservable characteristics. A drawback of this approach is that subjects may be upset if they arrive at the experiment site and are told that they cannot participate in the experiment. This can be compared to flight overbooking by airlines: it typically leads to unrest, animosity, and chaos, despite the fact that compensation is provided. Another potential drawback is that sometimes the subject pool may be scarce. As a result, there may not be sufficient numbers to assign some participants to the alternate category. We discuss issues related to attrition bias further in Chapter 4.

3. **Plan for (curious) nonparticipants.** It is important to be prepared for an interested audience composed of those who are not part of the experiment but are curious to know what is going on. This is particularly important when money is involved. Although nonparticipants may be distracting and at times even annoying, one must use tact in approaching these issues. One must be aware of specific cultural sensitivities and the status of certain individuals in society. Anecdotally, a coexperimenter and I politely turned a subject away from an experiment in order to ensure the privacy of other subjects. Later we learned that this subject was a fairly influential person in society and was badmouthing the experiment. So it was important to do some damage control in this circumstance. In particular, we had to explain that selection was random, and we also made a donation to the local school to express our appreciation for the community's cooperation.

4. **Beware of long sessions.** It is easy to try to address many issues during one experiment session, particularly considering subjects' high transportation costs. However, one must recall that the experimental task can be quite daunting for a less educated subject pool. So keep things simple and realistic. This is another reason that a pilot is useful; it will give you a good sense of the length of the experiment protocol. Remember that if subjects need to leave, for example, to attend to their livestock or engage in commercial activities, they will. So be realistic in terms of what can be achieved so that subjects will remain cooperative.

5. **Be aware of religious and cultural sensitivities.** This is particularly important in formulating one's protocol. Work closely with the translator ex ante to get a feel for what works and what does not. Are there colors, symbols, concepts (such as usury in Muslim law), and so on to which subjects might be sensitive? The experimenter should identify such issues ex ante and deal with them appropriately.

6. **Be prepared for distractions.** When participating in field experiments, subjects tend to be more disruptive than in laboratory experiments. Although one can certainly reiterate the importance of maintaining order, this may not be the cultural norm. For example, women with one or more children (in particular, crying babies) attending an experiment are more likely to participate when one is conducting experiments in rural areas. So one must be sensitive to such situations and not be distracted by them. One may upset subjects or even offend them by trying to keep strict order, and thus lose

BOX 2.5   Principles for designing an experiment: Practical suggestions

Experimenters should consider the following practices:

1. Conduct a pilot experiment. Pilot experiments are very informative and shed light on many complications that may arise during the actual experiment.

2. Plan for attrition among experiment subjects. One way to prepare for this is to recruit regular and alternate subjects.

3. Plan for (curious) nonparticipants. Members of the larger community who are not subjects might still be interested in the experiment; they should be treated with courtesy and tact.

4. Beware of long sessions. Do not address too many issues in a single experiment. Keep things simple, and have realistic expectations.

5. Be aware of religious and cultural sensitivities. Subjects might be sensitive to particular colors, symbols, or concepts (such as usury, in the case of certain Muslim communities).

6. Be prepared for distractions. A certain level of distraction (from children accompanying a subject, for example) might be unavoidable, so plan for this; holding multiple sessions, as suggested below, can help.

7. Hold two or more sessions for each treatment variable you test. This allows you to identify and allow for session-level differences such as nuisances or distractions that might affect all individuals participating in the session.

Source: Author.

experimenter control completely. So it is important to focus on the main issues at hand. To the extent possible, make note of such situations and test whether they matter in ex post analysis, for example, by tagging specific subjects and those who are around them in the experiment session. Controlling for session-level effects is also a possibility provided that more than one session has been conducted (more on this next).

7. **Hold two or more sessions for each treatment variable you test.** To have sufficient numbers in each treatment, it is likely that two or more experiment sessions will be required for each treatment. This will also help the experimenter to test or control for session-level effects, which may be important. Expect to conduct at most three two- or three-hour sessions per day. My experience has shown that

two such sessions are feasible, one before lunch and one after lunch. Anything beyond that is likely to be too ambitious because the field team typically needs a break for lunch. If one tries to do more, it is likely to lead to noncooperative behavior. Furthermore, the subjects may need breaks at specific times of the day. For example, in Muslim areas prayer is offered at specific times of the day, and one must work around that. So again be realistic and sensitive to the field situation. Finally, it is important to reserve a resting day in between every three days of conducting experiments; sessions are exhausting, and one does not want to start making unnecessary mistakes due to exhaustion.

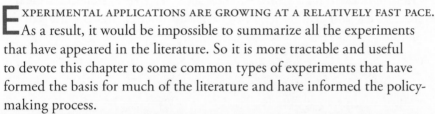

CHAPTER 3
Examples of Experiments

EXPERIMENTAL APPLICATIONS ARE GROWING AT A RELATIVELY FAST PACE. As a result, it would be impossible to summarize all the experiments that have appeared in the literature. So it is more tractable and useful to devote this chapter to some common types of experiments that have formed the basis for much of the literature and have informed the policy-making process.

In what follows, we discuss the following types of experiments: (1) ultimatum games, (2) dictator games, (3) trust games, (4) public goods (or prisoner's dilemma) games, (5) coordination games, (6) market experiments (auctions), and (7) risk- and time-preference experiments (for a summary of experiment types, see Box 3.1 at the end of this chapter). The rationale for conducting these experiments typically originated from the premise of testing the behavioral predictions of a theoretical framework. This is the first purpose for conducting experiments identified in Chapter 1.

The role of theory in the process of conducting economic research was addressed when discussing the rationale for experimentation. Basically, theory organizes our knowledge and helps us predict behavior in new situations. This goes back to—among others—Samuelson's (1947) discussion of *operationally meaningful theorems,* which he described as hypotheses about empirical data that could conceivably be refuted, if only under ideal conditions. Perhaps more important for experiments, theory tells us what data are worth gathering and suggests ways to analyze new data. As such, theory helps us design experiments.

Because many of the aforementioned types of experiments rely on some type of game, we will review certain concepts in the theory of games, economic behavior, and uncertainty. This said, game theory is just one set of tools that serves us well to "collect our thoughts." Ultimately, the model that best fits an experimenter's (and, more broadly, a researcher's) purpose depends on the research question under consideration and the reality at hand.

Not all experiments are for theory testing. As Smith (1982) and, more recently, Card, DellaVigna, and Malmendier (2011) discuss, experiments may be heuristic or descriptive (in the parlance of Smith and Card, DellaVigna, and Malmendier, respectively). However, even in the case of such experiments, typically the experimenter has some model or at least some hypothesis in mind when designing the experiment. This also applies to experiments conducted to elicit "unobservable" characteristics (the second purpose for conducting experiments, as identified in Chapter 1), to test for the sensitivity of experimental results to different forms of heterogeneity (the third purpose), or both.

Prior to proceeding, the interested reader is referred to some additional references that will give a sense of the experiments that are appearing in the economics literature:

1. The website www.fieldexperiments.com contains selected examples of research that incorporates experimental methods in different types of field studies, including RCTs.

2. The website http://en.wikipedia.org/wiki/Experimental_economics contains links to many experimental laboratories at universities, which point to experimental working papers on different topics.

3. *Experimental Economics,* the official journal of the Economic Science Association (ESA, the association of experimental economists), publishes experimental work of different types. Of course this includes only *part* of the published literature because experiments also appear in many other publication outlets, including more general-interest journals such as some of the American Economic Association journals, *Econometrica,* the *Quarterly Journal of Economics,* the *Review of Economic Studies, Economic Journal,* and *Economic Inquiry.*

4. The ESA's website, www.economicscience.org, also maintains archives of the association's most recent conferences. These links tend to take us to the programs of the meetings, which in turn give us a starting point for exploring some of the frontier of experimental work.

5. A recent initiative by the University of California–Berkeley and Norges Handelshøyskole (NHH, the Norwegian School of Economics), called the Symposium on Economic Experiments in Developing Countries (SEEDEC; see http://cega.berkeley.edu/events/SEEDEC2011/), provides a specific forum for researchers interested in conducting experiments of this type (that is, lablike field experiments) in a developing-country context.

EXPERIMENTS AND BEHAVIORAL GAME THEORY

Game theory comprises a set of analytical tools to help us understand the phenomena that we observe when decisionmakers interact. In other words, game theory is about what happens when people interact. Therefore, it constitutes a theory of *strategic interaction.* In practice, game theory is used for several purposes: to (1) predict how people *should* behave (a primary normative role), (2) explain how people *actually do* behave (a positive role), and (3) prescribe how institutions and policies should be designed considering the analysis performed under (1) and (2) (a secondary normative role).

There is still debate in the literature on the purpose of game theory and its usefulness for prescribing policy (see, for example, Rubinstein 2004). Our purpose here is not to make a case for or against game theory. Our discussion is intended to provide a background for more formally discussing certain experimental games.

The idea of a general theory of games was introduced by von Neumann and Morgenstern (1944), who proposed that most economic questions should be analyzed as games. Later Nash (1950) proposed what came to be known as the "Nash equilibrium" (discussed later). Since these seminal contributions were made to the field of game theory, there have been several other important developments. Some useful treatments of current concepts in game theory are those of Fudenberg and Tirole (1991), Gibbons (1992), Osborne and Rubinstein (1994), and Watson (2007). The reason we care about game theory for some of the discussion that follows is because it gives us a way to predict and test strategic behavior in certain contexts. This is the central interest of behavioral game theory (BGT), which is treated by Camerer (2003).[1] One way to think of BGT is as the study of how real agents, specifically human agents, behave when faced with strategic situations as proposed by game theory.

As Camerer (2003, 20) puts it, his book provides a long answer to a question game theory students often ask: "This theory is interesting . . . but do people actually behave this way?" And the answer is mixed. There are no interesting games in which subjects reach a predicted equilibrium immediately. And there are no games so complicated that subjects do not converge in the direction of equilibrium (perhaps quite close to it) with enough experience in the lab.

It is important to keep in mind what (of game theory) we are testing when we conduct game experiments. This argument has been made by Weibull (2004) and reiterated by Bardsley et al. (2010). The games and solution concepts described in traditional game theory are *abstract concepts.* In conducting an experimental test of a prediction derived from game theory (as we discuss further later), a typical approach is to construct a "laboratory" analogue of such an abstract game. This is what

---

[1]A survey of selected literature on experimental games is given by Chakravarty et al. (2011).

Weibull and Bardsley et al. refer to as a *game protocol* and an *implemented game,* respectively.

In such "real" games, concrete entities substitute for abstract concepts in the theory: real people serve as substitutes for theoretical agents, material payoffs (typically money) substitute for utilities, actual rules or institutions substitute for rules of the game, and so on. Assuming that such a game has the necessary correlates, one may derive predictions for it by applying some solution concept of interest, using the relevant concrete features of the implemented game as inputs. The degree of correspondence between these predictions and observed behavior in the implemented game then forms the basis of the experimental test. But such tests are joint tests of (1) the solution concept (such as the Nash equilibrium, discussed more later) and (2) any assumptions involved in connecting the concepts in the abstract and implemented games.

In what follows, we discuss some common experiment protocols, some of which are based on games (that is, strategic situations between two or more players, which can therefore be considered *implemented games* or *game protocols*) and some of which are based on nonstrategic, possibly individual, decisionmaking contexts (which can be considered *implemented models, scenarios,* or *frameworks* but are not games in the strict sense).

Our discussion of each protocol is organized quite mechanically:

1. We first discuss the theoretical construct (game or otherwise) and the key predictions that motivate the experiment protocol.

2. We then discuss some findings that have been reported in the literature. In this process, we also address how these findings have informed (or could inform) policymaking.

Those interested in conducting any of these experiments can perform a Google search by entering the key phrase "X instructions," where X stands for the type of game or experiment in question, for example, "ultimatum game instructions." These searches will return hits on papers that report the type of experiment in question. In turn, these can provide access to instructions or protocols (or both) used to implement the experiment in question. These instructions may be part of the actual paper, be posted on a linked website, or be available upon request. In what follows, at times the reader is pointed to hyperlinks to instructions for the experiment in question.

Finally, note that some of the discussion below draws heavily on Camerer (2003) and on Plott and Smith (2008). So the interested reader is referred to their texts for additional discussion.

ULTIMATUM GAMES

In an ultimatum game, one person, typically called the Proposer, makes a take-it-or-leave-it offer, dividing some amount of money between herself and another person. If the second person, typically called the Responder, accepts the division, both earn the specified amounts. If the Responder rejects it, they both get nothing. The ultimatum game was introduced by Güth, Schmittberger, and Schwarze (1982).

How are people expected to play this game? If Responders maximize their own earnings, they should accept the smallest allowable nonnegative payoff. On the other hand, if Proposers also maximize their own earnings and expect Responders to maximize theirs, they should offer the smallest allowable nonnegative amount. So if each player is motivated only by maximizing his own money payoff, any division can be supported as a so-called Nash equilibrium (NE) of the game, but there is a unique subgame perfect Nash equilibrium (SPNE) in which the Proposer offers a split that gives the Responder the smallest allowable nonnegative payoff and the Responder accepts.[2]

There is an extensive literature showing that behavior deviates from the SPNE in predictable ways: Responders frequently reject "low" offers, and Proposers commonly make proposals of close-to-even splits, despite the aforementioned predictions (see, for example, Davis and Holt 1993 and Camerer 2003). One possible interpretation of behavior in the ultimatum game is that it reflects the failure of individuals to apply backward induction reasoning. However, as discussed earlier, when we test game theory in an implemented game we are testing a joint hypothesis between the solution concept (in this case SPNE derived through backward induction) *and* any assumptions that tie together the game and its protocol counterpart— in particular, assumptions regarding people's preferences over their own and others' monetary payoffs. So if we move away from the standard assumption that each person only maximizes her own payoff, this opens a whole range of potential alternative explanations.

These explanations matter for what we infer from ultimatum game results. The dictator game, which is discussed further later, enables us to tease apart to what extent Proposers make "fair" offers in the ultimatum game due to fear of rejection or altruistic motives. Evidence seems to

---

[2]In game theory, the NE (see Nash 1950) is a solution concept of a game involving two or more players in which each player is assumed to know the equilibrium strategies of the other players and no player has anything to gain by changing only his own strategy unilaterally. A SPNE is a refinement of the NE applied to a dynamic or extensive form game; in particular, a strategy profile is a SPNE of a dynamic game if it is an NE for every subgame of that game. The SPNE is typically derived through a process called backward induction. For more formal definitions, refer to texts such as Osborne and Rubinstein (1994).

suggest that Proposers behave mostly out of fear and only a little out of altruism or fairness. Ultimatum games thus give us a sense of what people's bargaining preferences look like in a noncompetitive environment. To that extent, they can help inform policy by giving us a sense of prevailing social norms of fairness. These norms tend to be important, particularly for policy in rural areas, where they substitute for often missing legal institutions and property rights. Therefore, ultimatum games have been used to explore cultural differences in "fairness" norms across societies (see, for example, Roth et al. 1991 and Henrich et al. 2004) and to measure informal institutions (see Jakiela forthcoming).

This said, we should be cautious when interpreting findings from ultimatum games because the perceived fairness (possibly due to fear of rejection) seems to be context dependent. Roth et al. (1991) conducted a bargaining experiment (based on the ultimatum game) and a market experiment across different societies.[3] Despite the fact that equilibrium predictions were similar across these contexts, they found that behavior in the ultimatum game deviated from SPNE (as found in other studies), whereas behavior in the market experiment converged to equilibrium. They conjecture that this was due to cultural differences and that the competitive environment of the market experiment might trump the fairness concerns in players' preferences.

Examples of instructions for ultimatum games are available at http://cba .ua.edu/assets/docs/ppecorin/App.pdf and http://grace.wharton.upenn.edu/ risk/downloads/archive/arch333.pdf.

DICTATOR GAMES

A dictator game can be seen as an ultimatum game in which the Responder's possibility to reject the offer has been removed. In other words, the Proposer is "dictator" in the sense that whatever this player offers is "final." Because the Proposer's payoff does not depend on a subsequent action by the Responder, if a Proposer truly seeks to maximize her own money payoffs, she should take all and leave zero for the Responder. So the SPNE for the dictator game is that the dictator takes all. Due to the lack of strategic motives, the dictator game enables us to establish whether Proposers in ultimatum games make generous offers because they fear rejection or because they are purely altruistic.

Many studies have looked at behavior in dictator games, particularly what "giving" implies in these games and how that varies with different

---

[3] This study is also useful because its design also addressed several methodological issues that emerge when conducting experiments across different countries, such as experimenter, language, and currency effects.

types of variables and conditions (see Camerer 2003 for a review).[4] Broadly, dictator game giving is consistent with altruistic motives, which suggests that people care about others' welfare. These distributional preferences are relevant for policy because they give a sense of how people in society will treat others. For example, they can impact (1) how we formulate tax policy (consider politician–voter relations); (2) how we design contribution schemes, for example, for charitable organizations, social clubs, or farmer groups (consider grantor–beneficiary relations); and (3) how we plan for or deal with other welfare-reducing activities such as crime and social exclusion.

As in the case of ultimatum games, however, we should be cautious when interpreting findings from dictator games. List (2007), Bardsley (2008), and Jakiela (2011) all report that Dictators' preferences for sharing are dependent on the context of their choice, suggesting that dictator games might overstate altruistic motives. However, the latter study also found that Dictators' elasticity of substitution between their own and others' payoffs is not affected by such context dependence. This renders some validity to the conclusions drawn from dictator games.

Sample instructions for a simple dictator game protocol conducted as part of a pre-experiment listing exercise reported by Hill, Maruyama, and Viceisza (2012) are available at my website, http://sites.google.com/site/viceisza/research. Instructions for a more elaborate dictator game protocol are available at http://artsci.wustl.edu/~pjakiela/jakielaEESI_instructions.pdf; these instructions are associated with experiments reported by Jakiela (2011).

TRUST GAMES

As Arrow (1972, 357) states, "Virtually every commercial transaction has within itself an element of trust, certainly any transaction conducted over a period of time." More broadly, it can be argued that almost any activity between people requires trust. As a result, the level of trust in society plays a fundamental role in the policymaking process. Specifically, the prevalence of trust impacts the presence of (legal) institutions, the simplicity of engaging in (economic) transactions, political processes (such as voting behavior and elections), and so on.

In a trust game, as proposed by Berg, Dickhaut, and McCabe (1995) and earlier by Camerer and Weigelt (1988), the Trustor has X, which she can keep or send. Suppose she sends T and keeps $X - T$. The amount sent earns a return, at a rate $(1 + r)$, and becomes $(1 + r)T$. Then another player, the Trustee, must decide how to share the new amount $(1 + r)T$ with the

---

[4]Some of these studies are Forsythe et al. (1994), Andreoni and Miller (2002), List (2007), Andreoni and Bernheim (2009), and Jakiela (2011).

Trustor.[5] Suppose he keeps Y and returns $(1 + r)T - Y$. Then the total payoffs are Y for the Trustee and $(X - T) + (1 + r)T - Y$ for the Trustor.[6]

In this game, trust is the willingness to bet that another person will reciprocate a risky move (at a cost to himself). Trust is risky because once the Trustor sends, there is a probability that the Trustee will send nothing back. So, the amount sent is typically taken to measure trust, and the amount returned is taken to measure reciprocity or trustworthiness. If players maximize their earnings, reasoning by backward induction we assume that the Trustee will keep all. In turn, anticipating this, a self-interested Trustor will send nothing back. So the SPNE for the trust game is that neither trust nor trustworthiness is observed. Despite these predictions, Berg, Dickhaut, and McCabe (1995) found a substantial amount of blind trust in their experiments. This finding has been replicated by many other studies in different types of contexts (see, for example, Cox 2004 and Ashraf, Bohnet, and Piankov 2006).

To understand the role of trust games in the policymaking process, particularly with regard to farmers, consider a typical contract farming arrangement in which a firm contracts a farmer to deliver a certain quantity and quality of a product at a certain point in time for payment at a specified price (see, for example, Glover 1987; de Janvry, Fafchamps, and Sadoulet 1991; and Porter and Phillips-Howard 1997). These arrangements tend to be complicated because typically there is asymmetric information on both sides, and both parties may have incentives to renege on the contract when the specified time comes. So trust is likely to play a role in such relationships, and we might expect contract farming arrangements to be more likely to prevail in contexts in which there is a greater prevalence of trust. The trust game can be used in these and other contexts to test parties' propensities to trust, which in turn can be used to understand when certain types of arrangements or institutions are likely to prevail.

Karlan (2005) made a seminal contribution to the literature in this sense. In particular, he compared behavior in a trust game with that in subsequent microfinance participation. He found that those who are more trustworthy are also more likely to repay their loans, as one might expect if the trust game is capturing behavior that proxies trust. More important, perhaps, Karlan's findings suggested that behavior in the trust game was not just a mere artifact of the environment under consideration.

Torero and Viceisza (2011) explored variants of trust games to assess a priori the potential impact of proposed revisions to contract farming

---

[5]Note that the Trustee is playing a dictator game in which the amount to be allocated was determined by the Trustor.

[6]Sometimes this game is also referred to as the investment game.

arrangements. They found, similarly to previous researchers, that third parties significantly increase trust. However, potential collusion between the third party and the Trustee reduces trust when the Trustor is female. These findings are consistent with previous results on gender differences in preferences and decisionmaking (see, for example, Croson and Gneezy 2009) and are suggestive of factors (such as gender) that should be kept in mind when designing interventions at the RCT level.

Another question that has been studied is: How do norms of trust (and reciprocity) strengthen and unravel? Related to this, what are the determinants of trust and trustworthiness? These questions are relevant for policy because they may directly impact how we design certain institutions such as microfinance arrangements, contractual arrangements (such as transactions with traders, buyers, and input suppliers), and extension.

Ashraf, Bohnet, and Piankov (2006), for example, explored the determinants of trust and trustworthiness by combining data from trust and dictator games conducted in Russia, South Africa, and the United States. They found that expected trustworthiness accounts for most of the variation in trust, suggesting that people should believe in each other or the institutions in which they interact in order for trust to develop.

Hill, Maruyama, and Viceisza (2012) also combined data from trust and dictator games, but for a different purpose. By providing a random subset of Trustees with behavior in the dictator game, we were able to identify the effect of one's peers on oneself. We found that a norm of reciprocity quickly unravels when individuals make decisions while observing others. It appears that observed lack of reciprocity by some acts as a means to justify one's own propensity to be nonreciprocal. Our results suggest that there may be a benefit to rewarding reciprocity in institutional arrangements in which reciprocity has a personal cost and people can observe others' behavior. In particular, the findings suggest that investments that encourage reciprocity, perhaps particularly as a new institution develops, could engender substantial returns for market development.

Examples of instructions for conducting a trust game are available at my website, http://sites.google.com/site/viceisza/research; these instructions were implemented as part of Hill, Maruyama, and Viceisza (2012) and in the original article by Berg, Dickhaut, and McCabe (1995).

COOPERATION EXPERIMENTS: PUBLIC GOODS GAMES

In a so-called public goods game, each of N players can invest resources c_i from their endowment e_i in a public good that is shared by everyone and has a total per-unit value of m. Suppose that (1) $m < 1$, so that a player does not benefit enough personally to contribute for private gain; (2) $mN > 1$, so that all players' contributing is Pareto improving; and (3) Player i earns $e_i - c_i + m(\sum_k c_k)/N$.[7] Under these assumptions (that is, $m < 1/N$), the pay-off-maximizing outcome is to contribute nothing ($c_i = 0$). In other words, the NE for the simultaneous game in which all players choose how much to contribute at the same time is that everyone contributes nothing. If everyone contributed, however, the players would collectively earn the most.

Early experiments demonstrated that the group of players makes contributions to the public good early in an experiment, but that contributions decay over time (this was first demonstrated by Isaac, McCue, and Plott 1985). One of the subsequent challenges was to discover why any contribution was made at all and why it tended to change over time. To some extent, the literature is still sorting this out (see Plott and Smith 2008 for some discussion); however, some factors that have been studied include (1) calibration (from corner to internal equilibria), (2) spiteful and rewarding behavior (punishment and rewards), (3) the knowledge and experiences of group members (learning, search confusion, warm glow, reputation, and beliefs), (4) fundamental attitudes and types, and (5) individual characteristics.

Public goods games (and prisoner's dilemma games as a special case) are models of situations in which one player's action imposes a harmful externality on others. As a result, the public goods game has a vast set of applications in economics and the social sciences more broadly. Virtually, any group-based activity in which people can "free-ride" (that is, one individual's behavior can negatively impact another individual's welfare and vice versa) can be modeled as a public goods game. Therefore, the game has been applied to the study of phenomena ranging from pollution to community public goods (such as wells and springs) to contributions to social clubs and activities.[8]

For example, suppose we want to understand free-riding behavior in farmer groups. We could conduct public goods games with members of a sample of farmer groups and see whether behavior in the games predicts how the group functions on different types of aggregates. In this sense, the

---

[7] Essentially, the well-known prisoner's dilemma game can be seen as a special case of the public goods game with $N = 2$ players.

[8] A related game is the so-called common pool resource game. This game is similar to the public goods game except that the return on the investment account is determined differently. Specifically, if aggregate investment exceeds a given level, the return from the investment account becomes less than the individual's private return for not investing (see, for example, Ostrom, Gardner, and Walker 1994). This technicality aside, the flavor of the common pool resource game is similar. The game is intended to model scenarios in which one player's behavior creates a negative externality for the other. As the name suggests, the common pool resource game was constructed to study the use of common resources such as water and irrigation (for example, the upstream-downstream usage of rivers), fishing grounds, forests, and so on.

game gives us a measure of the propensity to cooperate within the group. Suppose further that we would like to know whether certain types of punishment, reward, or leadership schemes are likely to increase cooperation within the group prior to implementing them as treatments in an RCT. Having validated that behavior in the public goods game correlates with actual measures of cooperation (such as voluntary time spent working on the group's collective field), we can design variants of lablike public goods games to test the likely impact of these distinct mechanisms.

Barr, Packard, and Serra (2011) and Barr et al. (2012) both correlated behavior in a public goods game with actual behavior outside the lab to understand the behavioral mechanisms that underlie findings at the RCT level. The first study combined experimental and survey data from Albania and showed that behavior in the public goods game predicts participation in school-level elections of parent class representatives as well as district-level voter turnout in national elections. The second study also combined different sources of data collected in Uganda to explore whether community monitoring improves collective action. Using findings from public goods games, the researchers show that community monitoring interventions indeed improve collective action as proxied by behavior in the games.

Examples of instructions for conducting a public goods game can be found in the paper by Fischbacher, Gaechter, and Fehr (2002), available at www.iew.unizh.ch/wp/iewwp016.pdf.

COORDINATION GAMES

Coordination games are a formalization of the idea of a coordination problem, meaning situations in which all parties can realize mutual gains, but only by making mutually consistent decisions. In technical terms, coordination games are games with multiple equilibria that require "coordination." Predicting which of these equilibria will be selected is a complex problem in game theory. Camerer (2003) divides coordination games into three categories: (1) matching games, (2) games with asymmetric payoffs, and (3) games with asymmetric equilibria. In matching games, all equilibria have the same payoffs for each player. In games with asymmetric payoffs, players disagree about which equilibrium is best due to the asymmetry. In games with asymmetric equilibria, the players are symmetric but the equilibria are not. A game with this feature is the "stag hunt" game, which is sometimes also referred to as the "assurance game." Suppose two hunters are pursuing a stag that can be captured only by both of them. The stag has great value, and both players can benefit if they coordinate on hunting it. However, if each hunter has the alternative of hunting a hare individually, coordination on hunting the stag might fail because one of them, unbeknownst to the other, chooses to hunt the hare. In such a case, the hunter who chooses to pursue the stag (that is, chooses the risky action) will suffer.

Goeree and Holt (2000) and Crawford, Costa-Gomes, and Iriberri (forthcoming) review some evidence of strategic behavior in coordination games, among other issues. One main finding in the literature is that coordination failure seems to result from strategic uncertainty. Coordination games have been applied quite extensively in pure laboratory contexts (see, for example, Van Huyck, Battalio, and Beil 1990; Heinemann, Nagel, and Ockenfels 2009; and many other references). However, it seems that they have featured less prominently in lablike field experiments, despite their potential to inform policy.

Consider the example of farmer groups discussed previously. Suppose that a group enters into a contract with a buyer. In order to fulfill the contract, the group needs to deliver a certain quantity and quality of a product by a certain date. Most important, a sufficient number of group members need to produce (1) a certain amount and (2) a certain quality (in order for the group to meet the minimum quantity-quality combination required for the contract). An individual farmer's decision to produce as necessary and deliver to the group can be modeled as a strategy in a coordination game played with his fellow farmers. Namely, the payoff from delivering as required to the group will depend on whether others do the same. Suppose, for example, that an insufficient number of farmers deliver to the group and the group is forced to renege on the contract. In such a case, the individual farmer ends up incurring the cost. So he truly faces strategic uncertainty in the sense that he takes a chance that depends on the behavior of others in the group.

The Senegal component of the Working Together for Market Access project conducts RCTs with farmer groups and combines the resulting data with survey and coordination game data (elicited through surveys). These are used to test how internal group dynamics and beliefs (as measured by behavior in the coordination games) are impacted by training on the potential benefits (and costs) of collective action and, in turn, how these affect collective activities such as group commercialization. Although the study is still in progress, it is anticipated that the findings will inform policy toward strengthening collective action through farmer-based organizations.

This is one example how lablike coordination games can be used to guide policy decisions. Other potential examples are (1) coordination on technologies, (2) coordination on production standards (in order to obtain certification, for example), and (3) coordination on information sharing.

Examples of instructions for conducting a coordination game can be found in an article by Van Huyck, Battalio, and Beil (1990; see http://

economicscience.us/jvh/CRFAIL9.HTM#Download for the working paper version of their article, which contains the original instructions and data) and in Heinemann, Nagel, and Ockenfels (2009), whose instructions are available in the 2008 working paper version, available at www.finance .uni-frankfurt.de//wp/879.pdf.

MARKET EXPERIMENTS (AUCTIONS)

Some of the first experiments in economics were market experiments (Davis and Holt 1993). Chamberlin (1948) reported the first market experiment, in which he induced the demand and cost structures by dealing a deck of cards marked with values and costs to student subjects. Through trading, sellers could earn the difference between the cost they were dealt and the contract price they negotiated. Similarly, buyers could earn the difference between the value they were dealt and their negotiated contract price.

Trading in these markets was both unregulated and essentially unstructured. Students were permitted to circulate freely around the classroom to negotiate with others in a decentralized manner. Despite this "competitive" structure, Chamberlin concluded that outcomes systematically deviated from competitive predictions. In particular, he noted that the quantity of transactions was greater than the quantity determined by the intersection of supply and demand.

Later Vernon Smith, who had participated in Chamberlin's initial experiment as a Harvard graduate student, became intrigued by the method. He conjectured that the decentralized trading that occurred as students wandered around the room was not the appropriate institutional setting for testing the received theories of perfect competition. As an alternative, Smith (1962, 1964) devised a laboratory *"double auction" institution* in which all bids, offers, and transaction prices were public information. He demonstrated that such markets could converge to efficient, competitive outcomes, even with a small number of traders who initially knew nothing about market conditions. Thus Smith began to study the effects of changes in trading institutions on market outcomes. Since these initial market experiments, there have been many studies reporting behavior in market and auction institutions. Some are reviewed by Plott and Smith (2008).

The role of market experiments to inform policy is probably the most obvious. In almost any country, some type of market institution is present. Markets serve the purpose of centralizing information, establishing prices, and facilitating the trade of goods and services. Markets can play a particularly important role in the development of rural areas, where they can create surplus and help farmers escape poverty. In fact, one of IFPRI's

> ### BOX 3.1   Some common experiment types
>
> 1. Ultimatum game. One person, typically called the Proposer, divides some amount of money between himself and another person, making a take-it-or-leave-it offer. If the second person, typically called the Responder, accepts the division, each receives the specified amount. If the Responder rejects it, they both get nothing.
>
> 2. Dictator game. This is an ultimatum game in which the Responder's ability to reject the offer has been removed. The Proposer is Dictator in the sense that whatever this player offers is "final."
>
> 3. Trust game. The Trustor has X amount of money, which she can keep or send. If she sends some money (say, an amount T), keeping the difference $(X - T)$, the amount sent earns a return $(1 + r)$. Then another player, the Trustee, must decide how to share the amount received (that is, $(1 + r)T$) with the Trustor. Once the Trustee chooses to send all, some, or none of the amount received back to the Trustor, the game ends. If the Trustor decides at the outset not to send any amount to the Trustee, the games ends then.
>
>   The amount sent by the Trustor is typically referred to as "trust" because, once it is sent, there is no guarantee of receiving any money back. The amount returned by the Trustee is sometimes referred to as "reciprocity" because it is seen as a repayment of trust: the Trustee has no reason, other than motives such as altruism, to return any money to the Trustor.
>
> 4. Public goods (or prisoner's dilemma) game. Each player in a group has an equal amount of wealth. Each can invest part of this wealth in a common fund (the "public good") or in his private account (the "private good"). Whatever is put into the public good will be multiplied by a certain amount and divided evenly among all the players; whatever is put into the private good earns a private return. If everyone contributes to the public good, the group's total amount of wealth will be maximized (this can be considered a social optimum). However, an individual player can obtain greater personal wealth than the others by contributing everything to his

divisions has "markets" in its title, and one of its major research themes is to better understand how farmers can be linked to markets.

Market and auction experiments can help us understand farmers' bargaining and bidding behaviors, the role of information in impacting such behaviors, and those market or auction institutions that are most likely to function (and be understood) in rural areas. Lusk and Shogren (2007) review some of the literature on experimental auctions, particularly with applications in agricultural economics.

private good while all the other players contribute to the public good. So it makes sense to get a "free ride" from others' contributions to the public good.

5. Coordination game. There are several types of coordination games. They typically involve two players who can choose risky or safe actions. If both choose the risky action, they earn more than if they had played it safe. However, if one person does not choose the risky action, the person who *did* will earn less than if she had played it safe. One textbook example of a coordination game is a "stag hunt" game.

6. Market experiments (auctions). In a market experiment, players are typically assigned to the roles of buyers or sellers and simulate the trading of goods and services. Predetermined rules of trade are established, and convergence to market equilibrium, or failure to converge, is typically studied. Holding some kind of auction is one way of simulating a market among the players.

7. Risk- and time-preference experiments. The typical risk-preference experiment presents a subject with choices about lotteries—that is, scenarios that could lead to either a good or a bad outcome. The subject's choices are then used to infer his risk preference. The typical time-preference experiment presents a subject with choices about an amount of money he could receive in the near future and an amount of money he could receive in the more distant future. The subject's choices are then used to infer his time preferences (also referred to as patience). Risk- and time-preference experiments tend to be conducted together.

Source: Author.

The first chapter of Davis and Holt (1993; http://press.princeton.edu/chapters/s5255.pdf) contains a simple but concrete example of a market experiment. The appendix to that chapter (Appendix A1) contains a full set of sample procedures for conducting an oral double auction. Those interested in conducting such experiments can refer to the website or to their book (specifically, Chapters 3, 4, and 5) for details. Furthermore, www.econport.org and http://veconlab.econ.virginia.edu/admin.htm also provide access to different means of conducting web-based, or otherwise computerized, market experiments.

RISK- AND TIME-PREFERENCE EXPERIMENTS

At the foundation of neoclassical economics stand assumptions about individual behavior. Among these are assumptions about the decisionmaker's risk and time preferences. Indeed, as Harrison (2011) notes, welfare evaluation of any proposed policy with risky outcomes should take into account people's attitudes toward risk. As a result, risk- and time-preference experiments are possibly one of the most widely used types of lablike field experiments in economics. To some extent, the literature on risk preferences can be dichotomized into three types of studies (1) those that seek to elicit risk preferences, to estimate them, or both; (2) those that use findings of type 1 as an explanatory variable for some other behavior of interest; and (3) those that test different models of choice (such as theories of expected and nonexpected utility) under uncertainty. Thus far, lablike field applications have mainly concentrated on studies of types 1 and 2. So we mainly focus on examples that fall into those categories.

Many types of instruments have been used to elicit or estimate people's risk preferences. Interestingly, one of the first elicitations of risk attitudes in economics was a field study conducted by Binswanger (1980), who found that rural farmers in India exhibited fairly risk-averse preferences. Since Binswanger's study, many papers have been published, some of which are Harrison, Humphrey, and Verschoor (2010), Charness and Viceisza (2011), and de Brauw and Eozonou (2011).

There have also been many studies that have explored risk preferences as behavioral determinants of actual risk taking (for example, Dohmen et al. 2011 and Engle-Warnick, Escobal, and Laszlo 2011) or to disentangle behavior elicited in other contexts, particularly behavior exhibited in lablike experiments such as those investigating trust (see, for example, Bohnet and Zeckhauser 2004) and coordination (as in the Working Together for Market Access project, for example).

Related to risk preferences are time preferences. Apart from the fact that time preferences are of independent interest, the literature has shown that if preferences are concave rather than linear (that is, if people are risk averse rather than risk neutral), discount rates will be biased upward. In other words, risk and time preferences are connected. As a result, Andersen et al. (2008) measured both risk and time preferences for each subject using the procedure of Coller and Williams (1999) to elicit discount rates and the procedure of Holt and Laury (2002) to elicit risk attitudes in order to jointly estimate both risk and time preferences.[9]

Similarly to risk-preference experiments, time-preference experiments have been conducted to assess behavioral determinants of other types of behavior, possibly elicited through lablike-field-experimental results (see, for example, Ashraf, Karlan, and Yin 2006 and Giné et al. 2011).

---

[9]Andreoni and Sprenger (2012) avoid the bias of linear preferences by eliciting time preferences with convex budget sets, and Laury et al. (2012) propose and test a new method that elicits curvature-controlled discount rates that are invariant to the form of the utility function.

Those interested in conducting risk- and time-preference experiments can consult the supplementary material that was published as part of Andersen et al. (2008; see www.econometricsociety.org/ecta/supmat/6966_ instructions%20to%20experimental%20subjects.pdf) or the instructions pertaining to Laury et al. (2012), which are in the working paper available at http://excen.gsu.edu/workingpapers/GSU_EXCEN_WP_2012-05.pdf.[10]

---

[10] Those interested in the part of the risk literature that is geared more toward testing models of choice under uncertainty can refer to, for example, Cox and Harrison (2008) or Cox et al. (2010; the instructions are available at http://excen.gsu.edu/jccox/subjects.html).

CHAPTER 4

Inferences from Experiments

I N THEORY, DRAWING STATISTICAL INFERENCES FROM EXPERIMENTAL DATA is not much different than doing so from nonexperimental data. The same statistical and econometric techniques that one might use in more "standard" analysis can also be used here. In fact, often because the data are experimental, the type of analysis involved can be simple. To see why, let us recall some of the previous discussion on our rationale for conducting experiments.

Previously we saw that the type of experiment we conduct depends on the purpose of the experiment and the research question at hand. For example, many experiments are conducted to test some theoretical hypothesis and therefore construct a proper counterfactual in order to identify some treatment effect of interest. In such cases, using a between- or within-subject design (or both), the experimenters seek to identify the effects of different treatment conditions on the average subject. One can conceivably see these studies as more of a *reduced form*. On the other hand, other experiments are conducted with the intent to elicit or estimate aspects of preferences that are otherwise unknown, such as preferences for risk, time, altruism, and so on. One can conceivably see these studies as more *structural* in nature.

Whatever the type of experiment under consideration, one of the main "claims to fame" of experimental data is that analysis and inference using such data should be simple if the counterfactual is taken to be similar data that are nonexperimental. The rationale goes back to the issue of experimental control. Typically, when dealing with experimental data, by design the experimenter or econometrician has created an environment in which he has a better understanding of how the data have been generated. So data analysis should be "simple" or "easy" either because one has clear theoretical models underlying the experimental design (bringing us back to the role of theory in experimentation) or because one's design is so refined that it leaves little doubt as to why a particular effect is being observed.

So why do some resist or caution against experimental data and results? Typically, two main types of critiques can be raised: (1) critiques about external validity and (2) critiques about internal validity. Both issues have been discussed in the literature (see, for example, Friedman and Sunder 1994; Behrman and Todd 1999; Duflo, Glennerster, and Kremer 2007; Bruhn and McKenzie 2009; Falk and Heckman 2009; Bardsley et al. 2010;

Camerer 2011; Al-Ubaydli and List 2012; and the symposia in the *Journal of Economic Literature* and the *Journal of Economic Perspectives*). We discuss these further next.

EXTERNAL AND INTERNAL VALIDITY

External validity asks to what extent can the findings in one context generalize to a different (in this case, broader and less stylistic) context? Concretely, if we move from a lablike field experiment to an RCT, to a natural field experiment, or to a field context that is not necessarily experimental, will the estimates we report hold up? Are they robust across contexts, subject pools, and so on?

As mentioned previously, the extent to which external validity is a concern depends on the experiment's purpose and the research question. For example, when testing strict game-theoretic predictions with a sample of field subjects we may not be concerned about the generalizability of such results (see further discussions in Falk and Heckman 2009 and Camerer 2011). This said, if we want to infer policy implications from an experiment for other contexts, perhaps external validity becomes of greater concern.

External validity is closely tied to the representativeness of one's subject pool as well as the relevance of the experimental task vis-à-vis the naturally occurring environment. These concerns should remind us of the complementary role of surveys when inferring results from experimental data. Using measures elicited in a survey conducted on one's subject pool, one can assess whether the subjects in the experiment are (at least observably) similar to a broader subject pool, such as those in a census or a previously conducted survey that constituted a larger sample. In particular, as Falk and Heckman (2009) point out, because experimental findings generally rely on treatment differences, one must mostly worry about the interaction of the treatment effect with other variables when generalizing findings.

Another important aspect of external validity that specifically pertains to the types of experiments discussed in this guide relative to RCTs or field observational contexts is that subjects typically know that they are participating in an experiment. The fact that subjects know they are part of an experiment could be argued to add "artificiality" to the experimental task at hand, and therefore to introduce "bias." Unless we argue that an external power (possibly one's own moral conscience or a greater force) is always observing us, this type of scrutiny does not exist in a more naturally occurring environment.

To mitigate this effect, which is a type of experimenter effect, we can design experiments between subjects and try to identify effects across treatments. The logic is as follows: if there is indeed an experimenter effect, we would expect it to be present and approximately "equal" always. So if we design an experiment whose main conclusions follow from a comparison across treatments, we could argue that any such experimenter effect will be netted out. We should not underestimate the potential for this effect, particularly when conducting experiments in rural areas. This is what I like to term the "*mzungu effect*."[1]

Internal validity asks whether the data permit correct causal inferences. In other words, internal validity is a matter of proper experimental controls, experimental design, and data analysis. If we recall the list of potential confounding effects identified previously, internal validity breaks down if any of these effects is present and we fail to properly control for it through ex post analysis.

Consider an example. Suppose a researcher conducts an experiment between subjects by randomly allocating half the subjects to treatment A and half the subjects to treatment B. Ex post, the researcher compares the behavior of the average subject in treatment A against the behavior of the average subject in treatment B and finds an effect. The researcher might conclude that the treatment had an effect. Now suppose the researcher uses covariates within the experiment, covariates collected through a survey, or both to see whether the average subject in treatment A is observably *different* from the average subject in treatment B and finds that they are different. Then, in the absence of further manipulations of the data, the aforementioned treatment effect would be considered internally *invalid,* and thus, misleading. Namely, the differential effect could have occurred because of the treatment or because the average subjects in the two treatments are different.

External and internal validity are both important; however, *at worst* an experimenter should seek to have internal validity. In other words, it is important that the experimenter institute proper experimenter controls and engage in appropriate analysis so she can be confident in the estimates she reports. Just because a study reports "experimental" findings, this does not imply that these are internally valid; the ultimate burden remains on the reader to use those findings with caution and make inferences appropriately.

As stated previously, ensuring internal validity is a matter of proper experimental design (supported by a clear research question or hypothesis), control, and data analysis. Combining these three components to ensure

---

[1] *Mzungu* is the southern, central, and eastern African term for "person of foreign descent." The term was first used by Africans to describe early European explorers. In this context, it refers to the case in which an "outsider" walks into a village and runs an experiment, and thus it might elicit behavior that is not representative of "typical" decisionmaking because subjects have nonstandard expectations of such a person. Consider, for example, a case in which subjects expect that the experimenter's findings will inform local government policy or interventions by nongovernmental organizations.

internal validity is important, particularly when conducting field experiments. Namely, as the experimenter moves (from the lab) to the field and thus loses some control over the data-generating process, aspects that were unforeseen or unknown at the time the experiments were designed are more likely to pose a threat for internal validity. Sometimes, even if foreseen or known, budget limitations may restrict the experimenter's ability to rule out confounding factors by design. So it is important to have close interaction among one's experimental design, controls, and identification strategy a priori in order to be able to report internally valid estimates ex post. For further discussion, see Bruhn and McKenzie (2009) on pre-tests for internal validity and Behrman and Todd (1999) on post-tests of internal validity.

ECONOMETRIC REFERENCES

Because the nature of this guide is to provide a basis for conducting experiments (and not necessarily for conducting data analysis) and because there are several existing good econometric references, we provide some very light discussion here.

Traditionally, analysis using (lab) experimental data has not been very deep, most of the time for good reason. Because the data are experimental, most researchers are happy with reporting some summary statistics; means-comparison tests, full distribution tests, or both; and some graphs that satisfy the "eyeball" or "ocular metric" test (see, for example, the discussion on data analysis in Friedman and Sunder 1994). To the extent that one's experiment can be argued to be internally valid, these "simple" comparisons are typically fine. This said, if internal validity is in question, deeper analysis is required. One way to think about it is that if internal validity is threatened, we need to treat experimental data as if they were nonexperimental. The advantage is that because the data do emerge from an experimental setup, one can usually identify relatively easily the source of the threat. One such example is Hill and Viceisza (2012). Although the proper controls were instituted in the experimental design, weather draws, which were drawn live during the experiment, turned out to display degenerate patterns across treatments. So we had to exploit aspects of the difference-in-difference and panel nature of the design as well as the nearest-neighbor matching technique proposed by Abadie et al. (2004) to explore the robustness of the treatment effects.

Another aspect that may pose a threat to internal validity is attrition (as we discussed previously). If, for some nonrandom reason, people who were intended to participate in the experiment did not show up or drop out during the process and this is unbalanced across treatments, this type of attrition can introduce a bias in one's findings. In this case also, further data manipulation is required. For further discussion of attrition bias in experimental contexts and additional references on how to deal with this, see Duflo, Glennerster, and Kremer (2007) and the references within.

A possible to-do list for conducting ex post analysis on experimental data that were collected for the purposes of identifying a treatment effect would comprise the following steps:

1. Assess any attrition and, if it is nonrandom, the extent to which there may be any bias (see Wooldridge 2002; Duflo, Glennerster, and Kremer 2007; and the references within).

2. Assess any other compromises to internal validity that may result from sources other than attrition (see Behrman and Todd 1999 and the references within).

3. Check unconditional summary statistics and treatment effects, both pooled across treatments and disaggregated by treatment.

4. Draw inferences and conduct testing using both unconditional and conditional specifications. The conditional specifications should control for any compromises to internal validity that were identified in steps 1 and 2 (see Wooldridge 2002 for possible specifications).

5. Check for the robustness of the findings in step 4 by employing alternative specifications, measures, interaction terms, and so on.

6. Check for external validity by, for example, comparing such observable characteristics of one's sample as gender, education, and land size to the same characteristics in larger, similar samples (such as region-level censuses). Check to what extent these characteristics are confounded with the treatment (see Falk and Heckman 2009 for further discussion).

On the other hand, if the experimental data were collected for the purposes of eliciting "unobservable" characteristics, the approach taken would be different. One example is given by Andersen et al. (2008), who specify a structural model to jointly estimate risk- and time-preference parameters. Their estimations are made through maximum likelihood (see the supplement to their article for additional details).

More generally, there are many other econometric sources, including but *certainly* not limited to Deaton (1995), Cameron and Trivedi (2005), Angrist and Pischke (2009), Imbens and Wooldridge (2009; also available as NBER working paper 14251), and miscellaneous lecture notes by these same authors, available at the National Bureau of Economic Research website (see www.nber.org/WNE/).

CHAPTER 5
Conclusions

THIS GUIDE DISCUSSES SOME BASIC CONCEPTS RELATED TO THE rationale and methodology for conducting lablike field experiments in economics. It is not exhaustive but has provided a starting point for those who are unfamiliar with these types of experiments.

The guide is mainly backward looking and relies on previous work to tell its story. However, there are still many open questions with regard to lab-like field experiments. Three such questions are:

1. What are the implications of new approaches (such as neuroeconomics and virtual experiments) for lablike field experiments?

2. What methodological difficulties do these experiments face? For example, are they more prone to experimenter effects such as framing, house money, endowment, or Hawthorne effects?

3. What will be the main role of these types of experiments in informing policymaking?

All in all, these questions are quite vast and can be addressed only over time. So we pose them in the conclusion for consideration for future work. Answers to these types of research questions will sharpen our understanding of the role that lablike field experiments will be able to play in informing policymaking, particularly in developing countries.

References

Abadie, A., D. Drukker, J. L. Herr, and G. W. Imbens. 2004. "Implementing Matching Estimators for Average Treatment Effects in Stata." *Stata Journal* 4 (3): 290–311.

Abbink, K., and H. Hennig-Schmidt. 2006. "Neutral versus Loaded Instructions in a Bribery Experiment." *Experimental Economics* 9 (2): 103–121.

Al-Ubaydli, O., and J. A. List. 2012. "On the Generalizability of Experimental Results in Economics." Accessed June 2012. www.nber.org/papers/w17957.

Andersen, S., G. W. Harrison, M. I. Lau, and E. E. Rutström. 2008. "Eliciting Risk and Time Preferences." *Econometrica* 76 (3): 583–618.

Andreoni, J., and B. D. Bernheim. 2009. "Social Image and the 50–50 Norm: A Theoretical and Experimental Analysis of Audience Effects." *Econometrica* 77 (5): 1607–1636.

Andreoni, J., and J. Miller. 2002. "Giving According to GARP: An Experimental Test of the Consistency of Preferences for Altruism." *Econometrica* 70 (2): 737–753.

Andreoni, J., and C. Sprenger. 2012. "Estimating Time Preferences from Convex Budgets." *American Economic Review* (forthcoming).

Angrist, J. D., and J. Pischke. 2009. *Mostly Harmless Econometrics: An Empiricist's Companion.* Princeton, NJ, US: Princeton University Press.

Arrow, K. J. 1972. "Gifts and Exchanges." *Philosophy and Public Affairs* 1 (4): 343–362.

Ashraf, N., I. Bohnet, and N. Piankov. 2006. "Decomposing Trust and Trustworthiness." *Experimental Economics* 9 (3): 193–208.

Ashraf, N., D. Karlan, and W. Yin. 2006. "Tying Odysseus to the Mast: Evidence from a Commitment Savings Product in the Philippines." *Quarterly Journal of Economics* 121 (2): 635–672.

Bardsley, N. 2008. "Dictator Game Giving: Altruism or Artefact?" *Experimental Economics* 11 (2): 122–133.

Bardsley N., R. Cubitt, G. Loomes, P. Moffatt, C. Starmer, and R. Sugden. 2010. *Experimental Economics: Rethinking the Rules.* Princeton, NJ, US: Princeton University Press.

Barr, A., T. Packard, and D. Serra. 2011. "Is Turning Out to Vote a Public Good Contribution? Evidence from a New Democracy." Paper presented at the Economic Science Association Meeting, October 10–12, in Tucson, AZ, US.

Barr, A., F. Mugisha, P. Serneels, and A. Zeitlin. 2012. "Information and Collective Action in the Community Monitoring of Schools: Field and Lab Experimental Evidence from Uganda." Accessed March 7, 2012. http://sites.google.com/site/andrewzeitlin/research/m%26m.pdf?attredirects=0.

Beegle, K., J. de Weerdt, J. Friedman, and J. Gibson. 2010. *Methods of Household Consumption Measurement through Surveys: Experimental Results from Tanzania.* Policy Research Working Paper Series WPS5501. Washington, DC: World Bank.

Behrman, J. R., and P. E. Todd. 1999. *Randomness in the Experimental Samples of PROGRESA—Education, Health, and Nutrition Program.* Washington DC: International Food Policy Research Institute.

Berg, J., J. Dickhaut, and K. McCabe. 1995. "Trust, Reciprocity, and Social History." *Games and Economic Behavior* 10 (1): 122–142.

Binswanger, H. P. 1980. "Attitudes toward Risk: Experimental Measurement in Rural India." *American Journal of Agricultural Economics* 62 (3): 395–407.

Bohnet, I., and R. Zeckhauser. 2004. "Trust, Risk and Betrayal." *Journal of Economic Behavior and Organization* 55 (4): 467–484.

Bruhn, M., and D. McKenzie. 2009. "In Pursuit of Balance: Randomization in Practice in Development Field Experiments." *American Economic Journal: Applied Economics* 1 (4): 200–232.

Caeyers, B., N. Chalmers, and J. de Weerdt. 2012. "Improving Consumption Measurement and Other Survey Data through CAPI: Evidence from a Randomized Experiment." *Journal of Development Economics* 98 (1): 19–33.

Camerer, C. 2003. *Behavioral Game Theory: Experiments on Strategic Interaction.* Princeton, NJ, US: Princeton University Press.

————. 2011. "The Promise and Success of Lab–Field Generalizability in Experimental Economics: A Critical Reply to Levitt and List." Accessed March 8, 2012. http://papers.ssrn.com/sol3/papers.cfm?abstract_id=1977749.

Camerer, C., and K. Weigelt. 1988. "Experimental Tests of a Sequential Equilibrium Reputation Model." *Econometrica* 56 (1): 1–36.

Cameron, A. C., and P. K. Trivedi. 2005. *Microeconometrics: Methods and Applications.* Cambridge, UK: Cambridge University Press.

Caplin, A., and A. Schotter, eds. 2008. *Foundations of Positive and Normative Economics: A Handbook.* Handbook in Economic Methodologies Series, Vol. 1. Oxford, UK: Oxford University Press.

Card, D., S. DellaVigna, and U. Malmendier. 2011. "The Role of Theory in Field Experiments." *Journal of Economic Perspectives* 25 (3): 39–62.

Carter, M. 2008. "Inducing Innovation: Risk Instruments for Solving the Conundrum of Rural Finance." Accessed March 8, 2012. www.aae.wisc.edu/carter/Papers/Carter%20AFD_EUDN%20paper%20rev.pdf.

Chakravarty S., D. Friedman, G. Gupta, N. Hatekar, S. Mitra, and S. Sunder. 2011. "Experimental Economics: A Survey." *Economic and Political Weekly* 46 (35): 39–78.

Chamberlin, E. H. 1948. "An Experimental Imperfect Market." *Journal of Political Economy* 56 (2): 95–108.

Charness, G., and A. C. G. Viceisza. 2011. *Comprehension and Risk Elicitation in the Field: Evidence from Rural Senegal.* IFPRI Discussion Paper 1135. Washington, DC: International Food Policy Research Institute.

Coller, M., and M. B. Williams. 1999. "Eliciting Individual Discount Rates." *Experimental Economics* 2 (2): 107–127.

Cox, D. R., and N. Reid. 2000. *The Theory of the Design of Experiments.* Boca Raton, FL, US: Chapman & Hall/CRC.

Cox, J. C. 2004. "How to Identify Trust and Reciprocity." *Games and Economic Behavior* 46 (2): 260–281.

Cox, J. C., and G. W. Harrison, eds. 2008. *Risk Aversion in Experiments.* Research in Experimental Economics, Vol. 12. Bingley, UK: Emerald.

Cox, J. C., V. Sadiraj, B. Vogt, and U. Dasgupta. 2010. "Is There a Plausible Theory for Decision under Risk? A Dual Calibration Critique." Accessed March 8, 2012. http://excen.gsu.edu/workingpapers/GSU_EXCEN_WP_2010-06.pdf.

Crawford, V. P., M. A. Costa-Gomes, and N. Iriberri. Forthcoming. "Structural Models of Nonequilibrium Strategic Thinking: Theory, Evidence, and Applications." *Journal of Economic Literature.*

Croson, R. T., and U. Gneezy. 2009. "Gender Differences in Preferences." *Journal of Economic Literature* 47 (2): 1–27.

Davis, D. D., and C. A. Holt. 1993. *Experimental Economics.* Princeton, NJ, US: Princeton University Press.

de Brauw, A., and P. Eozonou. 2011. *Measuring Risk Attitudes among Mozambican Farmers.* IFPRI Harvest Plus Working Paper 6. Washington, DC: International Food Policy Research Institute.

de Janvry, A., M. Fafchamps, and E. Sadoulet. 1991. "Peasant Household Behaviour with Missing Markets: Some Paradoxes Explained." *Economic Journal* 101 (November): 1400–1417.

Deaton, A. 1995. "Data and Econometric Tools for Development Analysis." In *Handbook of Development Economics,* ed. J. Behrman and T. N. Srinivasan. Amsterdam: Elsevier Science.

Dohmen, T., A. Falk, D. Huffman, U. Sunde, J. Schupp, and G. G. Wagner. 2011. "Individual Risk Attitudes: Measurement, Determinants and Behavioral Consequences." *Journal of the European Economic Association* 9 (3): 522–550.

Duflo, E., R. Glennerster, and M. Kremer. 2007. "Using Randomization in Development Economics Research: A Toolkit." In *Handbook of Development Economics,* ed. T. P. Schultz and J. Strauss. Amsterdam: Elsevier Science.

Engle-Warnick, J., J. Escobal, and S. Laszlo. 2011. "Ambiguity Aversion and Portfolio Choice in Small-Scale Peruvian Farming." *B. E. Journal of Economic Analysis and Policy* 11 (1): 68.

Falk, A., and J. J. Heckman. 2009. "Lab Experiments Are a Major Source of Knowledge in the Social Sciences." *Science* 326 (5952): 535–538.

Fischbacher, U. 2007. "Z-Tree: Zurich Toolbox for Ready-Made Economic Experiments." *Experimental Economics* 10 (2): 171–178.

Fischbacher, U., S. Gaechter, and E. Fehr. 2002. "Are People Conditionally Cooperative? Evidence from a Public Goods Experiment." *Economics Letters* 71 (3): 397–404.

Forsythe, R., J. L. Horowitz, N.E. Savin, and M. Sefton. 1994. "Fairness in Simple Bargaining Experiments." *Games and Economic Behavior* 6 (3): 347–369.

Fréchette, G., and A. Schotter, eds. Forthcoming. *The Methods of Modern Experimental Economics.* Handbook in Economic Methodologies Series, Vol. 2. Oxford, UK: Oxford University Press.

Friedman, D., and A. Cassar. 2004. *Economics Lab: An Intensive Course in Experimental Economics.* New York: Routledge.

Friedman, D., and S. Sunder. 1994. *Experimental Methods: A Primer for Economists.* Cambridge, UK: Cambridge University Press.

Fudenberg, D., and J. Tirole. 1991. *Game Theory.* Cambridge, MA, US: MIT Press.

Ganzach, Y., and N. Karsahi. 1995. "Message Framing and Buying Behavior: A Field Experiment." *Journal of Business Research* 32 (1): 11–17.

Gibbons, R. 1992. *Game Theory for Applied Economists.* Princeton, NJ, US: Princeton University Press.

Giné, X., P. Jakiela, D. Karlan, and J. Morduch. 2010. "Microfinance Games." *American Economic Journal: Applied Economics* 2 (3): 60–95.

Giné, X., J. Goldberg, D. Silverman, and D. Yang. 2011. "Revising Commitments: Field Evidence on the Adjustment of Prior Choices. Accessed March 8, 2012. www.personal.umich.edu/~deanyang/papers/gine%20goldberg%20silverman%20 yang%20-%20revising%20commitment.pdf.

Glover, D. 1987. "Increasing Benefits to Smallholders from Contract Farming: Problems for Farmers." *World Development* 15 (4): 441–448.

Goeree, J., and C. A. Holt. 2000. "Coordination Games." In *Encyclopedia of Cognitive Science,* ed. L. Nadel. New York: John Wiley & Sons.

Grosh, M. E., and P. Glewwe. 2000. *Designing Household Survey Questionnaires for Developing Countries: Lessons from 15 Years of the Living Standards Measurement Study,* Vols. 1, 2, and 3. Washington, DC: World Bank.

Grosh, M. E., and J. Muñoz. 1996. *A Manual for Planning and Implementing the Living Standards Measurement Study Survey.* LSMS Working Paper 126. Washington, DC: World Bank.

Güth, W., R. Schmittberger, and B. Schwarze. 1982. "An Experimental Analysis of Ultimatum Bargaining." *Journal of Economic Behavior and Organization* 3 (4): 367–388.

Haavelmo, T. 1958. "The Role of the Econometrician in the Advancement of Economic Theory." *Econometrica* 26 (3): 351–357.

Harrison, G. W. 2011. "Experimental Methods and the Welfare Evaluation of Policy Lotteries." *European Review of Agricultural Economics* 38 (3): 335–360.

Harrison, G. W., and J. A. List. 2004. "Field Experiments." *Journal of Economic Literature* 42 (4): 1009–1055.

Harrison, G. W., and E. E. Rutström. 2008. "Experimental Evidence on the Existence of Hypothetical Bias in Value Elicitation Methods." In *Handbook of Experimental Economics Results,* ed. C. R. Plott and V. L. Smith. Amsterdam: North-Holland.

Harrison, G. W., S. J. Humphrey, and A. Verschoor. 2010. "Choice under Uncertainty: Evidence from Ethiopia, India, and Uganda." *Economic Journal* 120 (543): 80–104.

Heinemann, F., R. Nagel, and P. Ockenfels. 2009. "Measuring Strategic Uncertainty in Coordination Games." *Review of Economic Studies* 76 (1): 181–221.

Henrich, J., R. Boyd, S. Bowles, C. Camerer, E. Fehr, and H. Gintis. 2004. *Foundations of Human Sociality: Economic Experiments and Ethnographic Evidence from Fifteen Small-Scale Societies.* New York: Oxford University Press.

Hill, R. V., and A. Viceisza. 2012. "A Field Experiment on the Impact of Weather Shocks and Insurance on Risky Investment." *Experimental Economics* 15 (2): 341–371. http://dx.doi.org/10.1007/s10683-011-9303-7.

Hill, R. V., E. Maruyama, and A. Viceisza. 2012. "Breaking the Norm: An Empirical Investigation into the Unraveling of Good Behavior." *Journal of Development Economics* 99 (1): 150–162. http://dx.doi.org/10.1016/j.jdeveco.2011.11.004.

Himelein, K. 2011. "Practical Sampling for Impact Evaluations." Accessed June 1, 2012. http://siteresources.worldbank.org/INTPOVRES/Resources/477227-1142020443961/2311843-1142870725726/2337154-1298126631524/Module2-9-SamplingforPIES%28KristenHimelein%29.pdf.

Hoffman, E., K. McCabe, and V. L. Smith. 1996. "Social Distance and Other-Regarding Behavior in Dictator Games." *American Economic Review* 86 (3): 653–660.

Hoffman, E., K. McCabe, K. Shachat, and V. L. Smith. 1994. "Preferences, Property Rights, and Anonymity in Bargaining Games." *Games and Economic Behavior* 7 (3): 346–380.

Holt, C. A., and S. K. Laury. 2002. "Risk Aversion and Incentive Effects." *American Economic Review* 92 (5): 1644–1655.

Imbens, G. M., and J. M. Wooldridge. 2009. "Recent Developments in the Econometrics of Program Evaluation." *Journal of Economic Literature* 47 (1): 5–86.

Isaac, R. M., K. F. McCue, and C. R. Plott. 1985. "Public Goods Provision in an Experimental Environment." *Journal of Public Economics* 26 (1): 51–74.

Jakiela, P. 2011. "Equity vs. Efficiency vs. Self-Interest: On the Use of Dictator Games to Measure Distributional Preferences." Accessed March 8. 2012. http://pamjakiela .com/jakielaEESI_15may11.pdf.

———. Forthcoming. "Using Economic Experiments to Measure Informal Institutions." In *Economic Institutions, Rights, Growth, and Sustainability: The Legacy of Douglass North,* ed. S. Galiani and I. Sened. Cambridge, UK: Cambridge University Press.

Jamison, J., and D. Karlan. 2011. "Measuring Preferences and Predicting Outcomes." Paper presented at the Symposium on Economic Experiments in Developing Countries, December 1–3, in Berkeley, CA, US.

Jamison, J., D. Karlan, and L. Schechter. 2008. "To Deceive or Not to Deceive: The Effect of Deception on Behavior in Future Laboratory Experiments." *Journal of Economic Behavior & Organization* 68 (3–4): 477–488.

Kagel, J., and A. Roth. 1997. *Handbook of Experimental Economics.* Princeton, NJ, US: Princeton University Press.

Karlan, D. 2005. "Using Experimental Economics to Measure Social Capital and Predict Financial Decisions." *American Economic Review* 95 (5): 1688–1699.

Khandker, S. R., G. B. Koolwal, and H. A. Samad. 2010. *Handbook on Impact Evaluation: Quantitative Methods and Practices.* Washington, DC: World Bank.

Laury, S., and C. Holt. 2008. "Payoff Scale Effects and Risk Preference under Real and Hypothetical Conditions." In *Handbook of Experimental Economics Results,* ed. C. R. Plott and V. L. Smith. Amsterdam: North-Holland.

Laury, S. K., M. M. McInnes, J. T. Swarthout, and E. Von Nessen. 2012. "Avoiding the Curves: Direct Elicitation of Time Preferences." Accessed June 4. http://excen.gsu .edu/workingpapers/GSU_EXCEN_WP_2012-05.pdf.

Levin, I. P., S. L. Schneider, and G. J. Gaeth. 1998. "All Frames Are Not Created Equal: A Typology and Critical Analysis of Framing Effects." *Organizational Behavior and Human Decision Processes* 76 (2): 149–188.

List, J. A. 2007. "On the Interpretation of Giving in Dictator Games." *Journal of Political Economy* 115 (3): 482–492.

———. 2011. "Why Economists Should Conduct Field Experiments and 14 Tips for Pulling One Off." *Journal of Economic Perspectives* 25 (3): 3–16.

Lusk, J. L., and J. F. Shogren. 2007. *Experimental Auctions: Methods and Applications in Economics and Marketing Research.* Cambridge, UK: Cambridge University Press.

Mookherjee, D. 2005. "Is There Too Little Theory in Development Economics Today?" *Economic and Political Weekly* 40 (40): 4328–4333.

Nash, J. 1950. "Equilibrium Points in *n*-Person Games." *Proceedings of the National Academy of Sciences* 36 (1): 48–49.

Osborne, M. J., and A. Rubinstein. 1994. *A Course in Game Theory.* Cambridge, MA: MIT Press. http://theory.economics.utoronto.ca/books/.

Ostrom, E., R. Gardner, and J. Walker. 1994. *Rules, Games, and Common Pool Resources.* Ann Arbor, MI, US: University of Michigan Press.

Plott, C. R. 1982. "Industrial Organization Theory and Experimental Economics." *Journal of Economic Literature* 20 (4): 1485–1527.

Plott, C. R., and V. L. Smith, eds. 2008. *Handbook of Experimental Economics Results.* Amsterdam: North-Holland.

Porter, G., and K. Phillips-Howard. 1997. "Comparing Contracts: An Evaluation of Contract Farming Schemes in Africa." *World Development* 25 (2): 227–238.

Roth, A. E., V. Prasnikar, M. Okuno-Fujiwara, and S. Zamir. 1991. "Bargaining and Market Behavior in Jerusalem, Ljubljana, Pittsburgh, and Tokyo: An Experimental Study." *American Economic Review* 81 (5): 1068–1095.

Rubinstein, A. 2004. Afterword to *Theory of Games and Economic Behavior: Sixtieth Anniversary Edition,* by J. von Neumann and O. Morgenstern. Princeton, NJ, US: Princeton University Press.

Samuelson, L. 2005. "Economic Theory and Experimental Economics." *Journal of Economic Literature* 43 (1): 65–107.

Samuelson, P. 1947. *Foundations of Economic Analysis.* Cambridge, MA, US: Harvard University Press.

Sandmo, A. 1971. "On the Theory of the Competitive Firm under Price Uncertainty." *American Economic Review* 61 (1): 65–73.

Smith, V. L. 1962. "An Experimental Study of Competitive Market Behavior." *Journal of Political Economy* 70 (2): 111–137.

———. 1964. The Effect of Market Organization on Competitive Equilibrium." *Quarterly Journal of Economics* 78 (2): 181–201.

———. 1976. "Experimental Economics: Induced Value Theory." *American Economic Review* 66 (2): 274–279.

———. 1982. "Microeconomic Systems as Experimental Science." *American Economic Review* 72 (5): 923–995.

Spybrook, J., H. Bloom, R. Congdon, C. Hill, A. Martinez, and S. W. Raudenbush. 2011. "Optimal Design Plus Empirical Evidence: Documentation for the 'Optimal Design' Software." Accessed June 4, 2012. http://pikachu.harvard.edu/od/.

Torero, M., and A. C. G. Viceisza. 2011. *Potential Collusion and Trust: Evidence from a Field Experiment in Vietnam.* IFPRI Discussion Paper 1100. Washington, DC: International Food Policy Research Institute.

———. 2012. "To Remit, or Not to Remit: That Is the Question: A Remittance Field Experiment." Accessed March 8. https://sites.google.com/site/viceisza/research.

Train, K., and W. Wilson. 2008. "Estimation on Stated-Preference Experiments Constructed from Revealed-Preference Choices." *Transportation Research Part B: Methodological* 42 (3): 191–203.

Van Huyck, J. B., R. C. Battalio, and R. O. Beil. 1990. "Tacit Coordination Games, Strategic Uncertainty, and Coordination Failure." *American Economic Review* 80 (1): 234–248.

von Neumann, J., and O. Morgenstern. 1944. *The Theory of Games and Economic Behavior.* Princeton, NJ, US: Princeton University Press.

Watson, J. 2007. *Strategy: An Introduction to Game Theory,* 2nd ed. New York: W. W. Norton.

Weibull, J. 2004. "Testing Game Theory." In *Advances in Understanding Strategic Behaviour: Game Theory, Experiments and Bounded Rationality: Essays in Honour of Werner Güth,* ed. S. Huck. Basingstoke, UK: Palgrave Macmillan.

Wooldridge, J. M. 2002. *Econometric Analysis of Cross Section and Panel Data.* Cambridge, MA, US: MIT Press.

Zwane, A. P., J. Zinman, E. Van Dusen, W. Pariente, C. Null, E. Miguel, M. Kremer, D. S. Karlan, R. Hornbeck, X. Giné, E. Duflo, F. Devoto, B. Crepo, and A. Banerjee. 2011. "Being Surveyed Can Change Later Behavior and Related Parameter Estimates." *Proceedings of the National Academy of Sciences* 108 (5): 1821–1826.

About the Author

Angelino C. G. Viceisza (A.Viceisza@cgiar.org) was a research fellow in the Markets, Trade, and Institutions Division of the International Food Policy Research Institute, Washington, DC, at the time he wrote this work. He is currently an assistant professor in the Department of Economics at Spelman College, Atlanta. His publications include "Breaking the Norm: An Empirical Investigation into the Unraveling of Good Behavior," *Journal of Development Economics* 99 (1), coauthored with Ruth Vargas Hill and Eduardo Maruyama, and "A Field Experiment on the Impact of Weather Shocks and Insurance on Risky Investment," *Experimental Economics* 15 (2), coauthored with Ruth Vargas Hill.

Index

Page numbers for entries occurring in boxes are followed by a *b;* those for entries in figures, by an *f;* and those for entries in notes, by an *n.*